HISTORY TIPSTERS

SNEAK INTO THE OVAL OFFICE

THE INSIDE SCOOP ON THE U.S. PRESIDENCY

WRITTEN BY BLAKE HOENA

ILLUSTRATED BY MANUEL MOLVAR

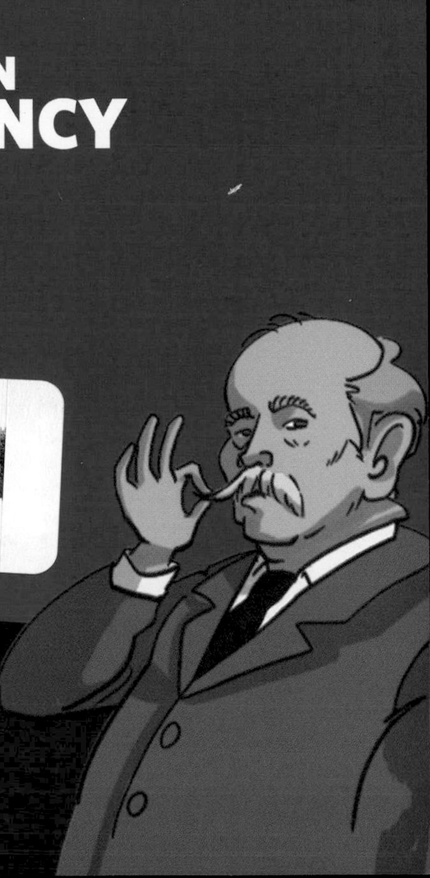

CAPSTONE PRESS
a capstone imprint

Published by Capstone Press, an imprint of Capstone
1710 Roe Crest Drive, North Mankato, Minnesota 56003
capstonepub.com

Library of Congress Cataloging-in-Publication Data is available on the Library of Congress website.

ISBN: 9781669076353 (hardcover)
ISBN: 9781669076308 (paperback)
ISBN: 9781669076315 (ebook PDF)

Summary: Playful graphics and text take readers on a historical tour of the presidents of the United States,
including lesser-known inside information.

Editorial Credits
Editor: Mandy Robbins; Designer: Heidi Thompson; Production Specialist: Tori Abraham

CONTENTS

INTRODUCTION: THE OVAL OFFICE

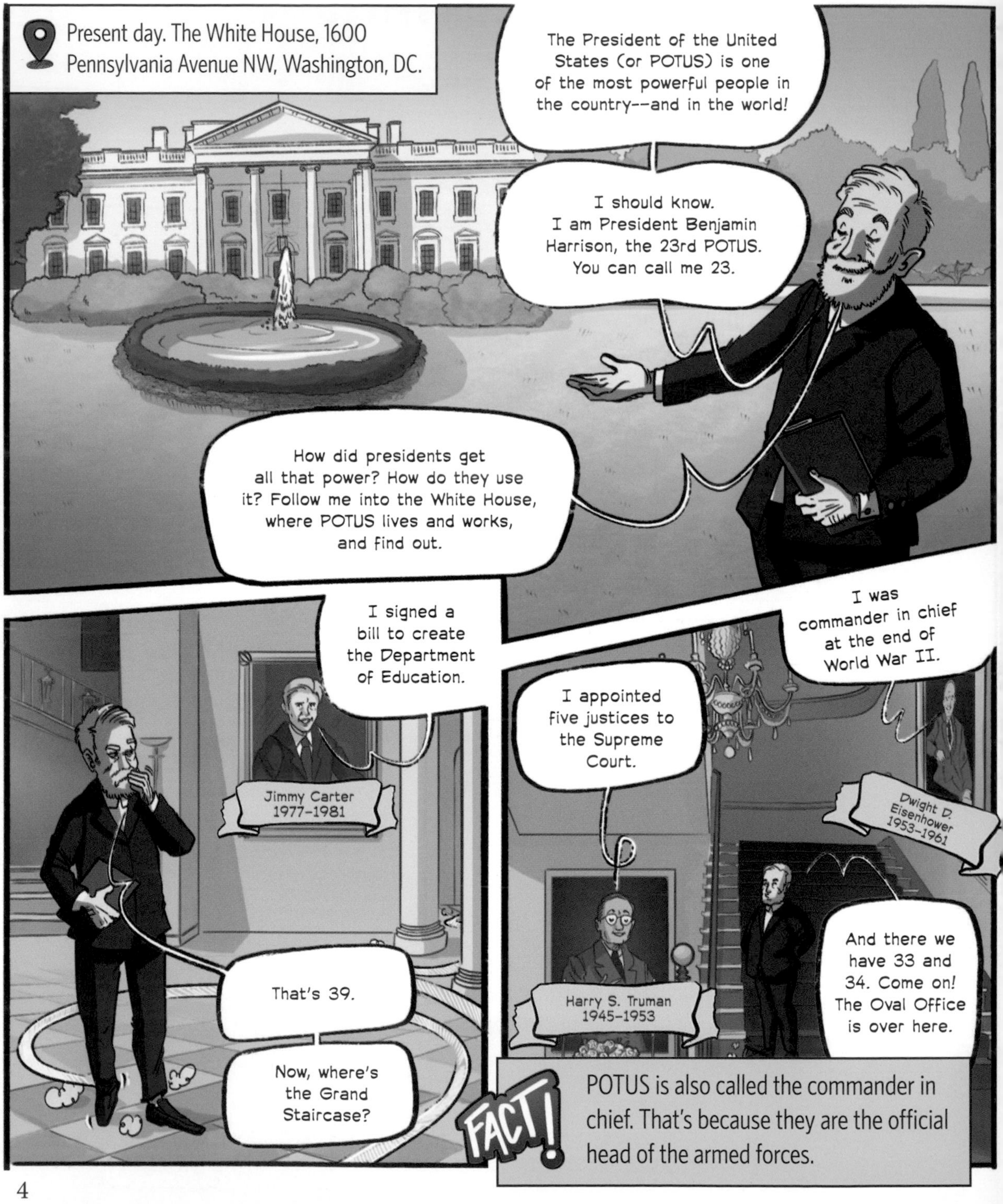

Present day. The White House, 1600 Pennsylvania Avenue NW, Washington, DC.
The President of the United States (or POTUS) is one of the most powerful people in the country--and in the world!
I should know. I am President Benjamin Harrison, the 23rd POTUS. You can call me 23.
How did presidents get all that power? How do they use it? Follow me into the White House, where POTUS lives and works, and find out.
I signed a bill to create the Department of Education.
Jimmy Carter 1977–1981
That's 39.
Now, where's the Grand Staircase?
I was commander in chief at the end of World War II.
I appointed five justices to the Supreme Court.
Dwight D. Eisenhower 1953–1961
Harry S. Truman 1945–1953
And there we have 33 and 34. Come on! The Oval Office is over here.

FACT! POTUS is also called the commander in chief. That's because they are the official head of the armed forces.

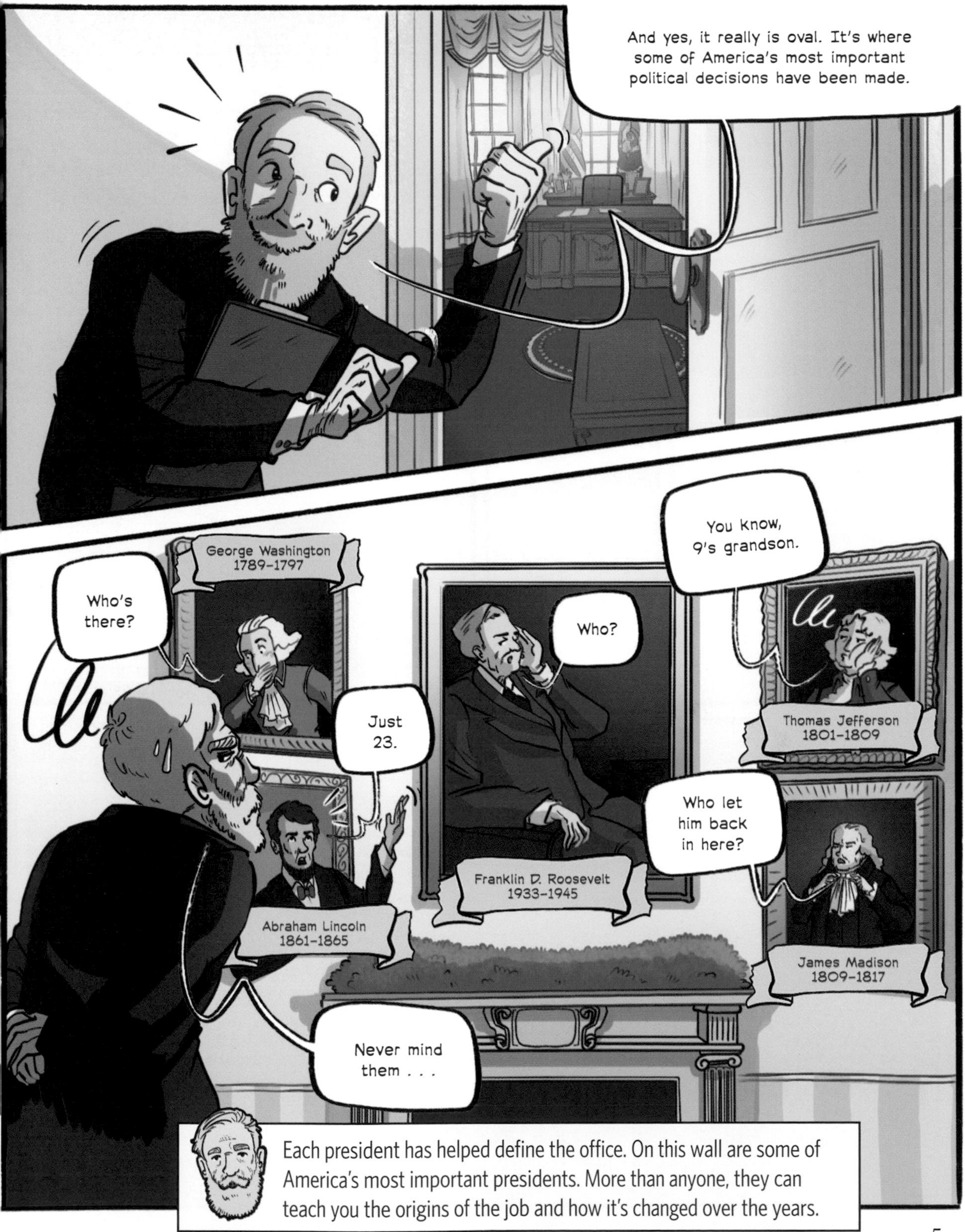
And yes, it really is oval. It's where some of America's most important political decisions have been made.
George Washington 1789–1797
Who's there?
Who?
Franklin D. Roosevelt 1933–1945
You know, 9's grandson.
Thomas Jefferson 1801–1809
Just 23.
Abraham Lincoln 1861–1865
Who let him back in here?
James Madison 1809–1817
Never mind them . . .
Each president has helped define the office. On this wall are some of America's most important presidents. More than anyone, they can teach you the origins of the job and how it's changed over the years.

CHAPTER ONE: THE FIRST PRESIDENT

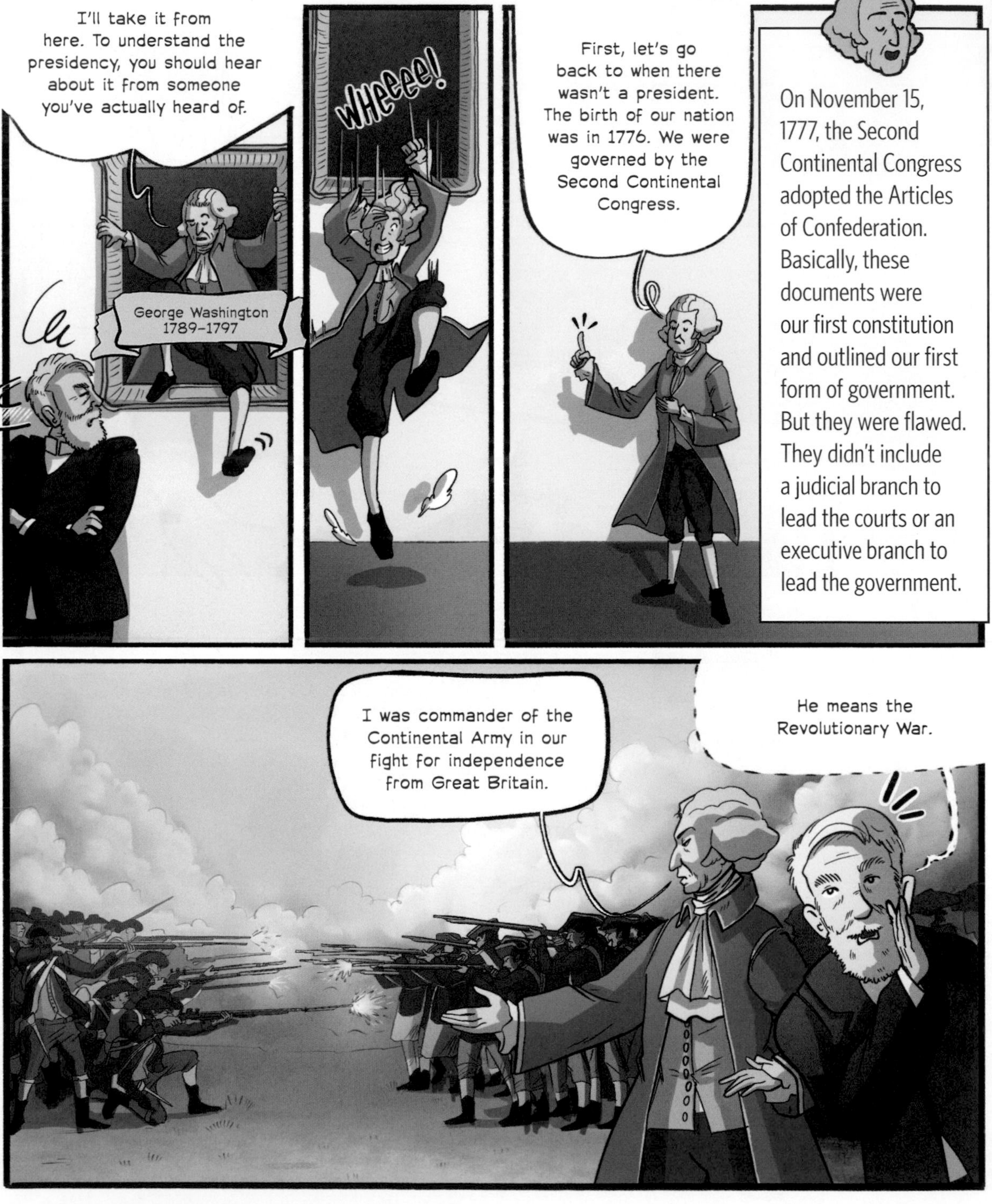

I'll take it from here. To understand the presidency, you should hear about it from someone you've actually heard of.
George Washington 1789–1797
WHeeee!
First, let's go back to when there wasn't a president. The birth of our nation was in 1776. We were governed by the Second Continental Congress.
On November 15, 1777, the Second Continental Congress adopted the Articles of Confederation. Basically, these documents were our first constitution and outlined our first form of government. But they were flawed. They didn't include a judicial branch to lead the courts or an executive branch to lead the government.
I was commander of the Continental Army in our fight for independence from Great Britain.
He means the Revolutionary War.

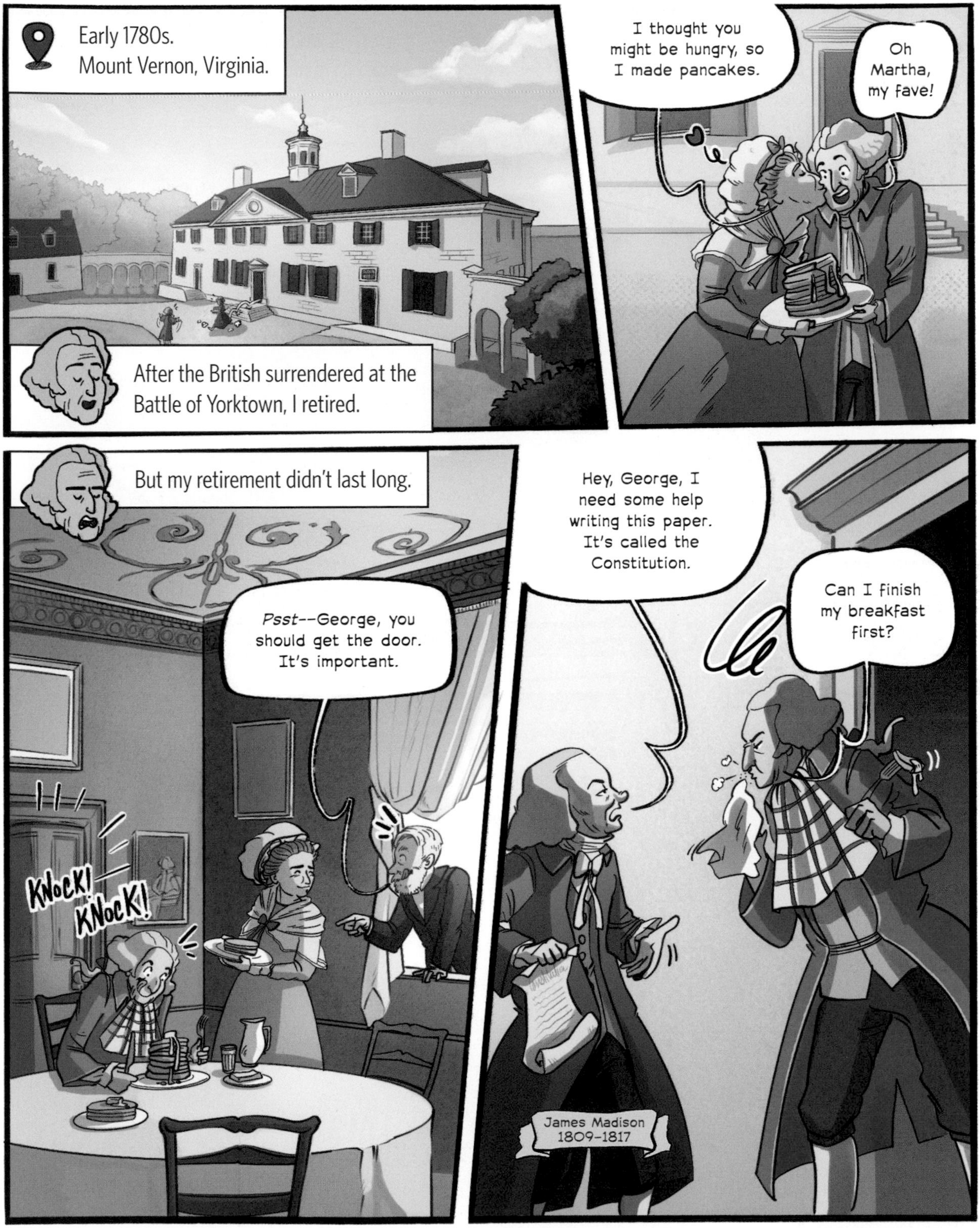
Early 1780s.
Mount Vernon, Virginia.
After the British surrendered at the Battle of Yorktown, I retired.
I thought you might be hungry, so I made pancakes.
Oh Martha, my fave!
But my retirement didn't last long.
Psst--George, you should get the door. It's important.
KNOCK! KNOCK!
Hey, George, I need some help writing this paper. It's called the Constitution.
Can I finish my breakfast first?
James Madison
1809–1817

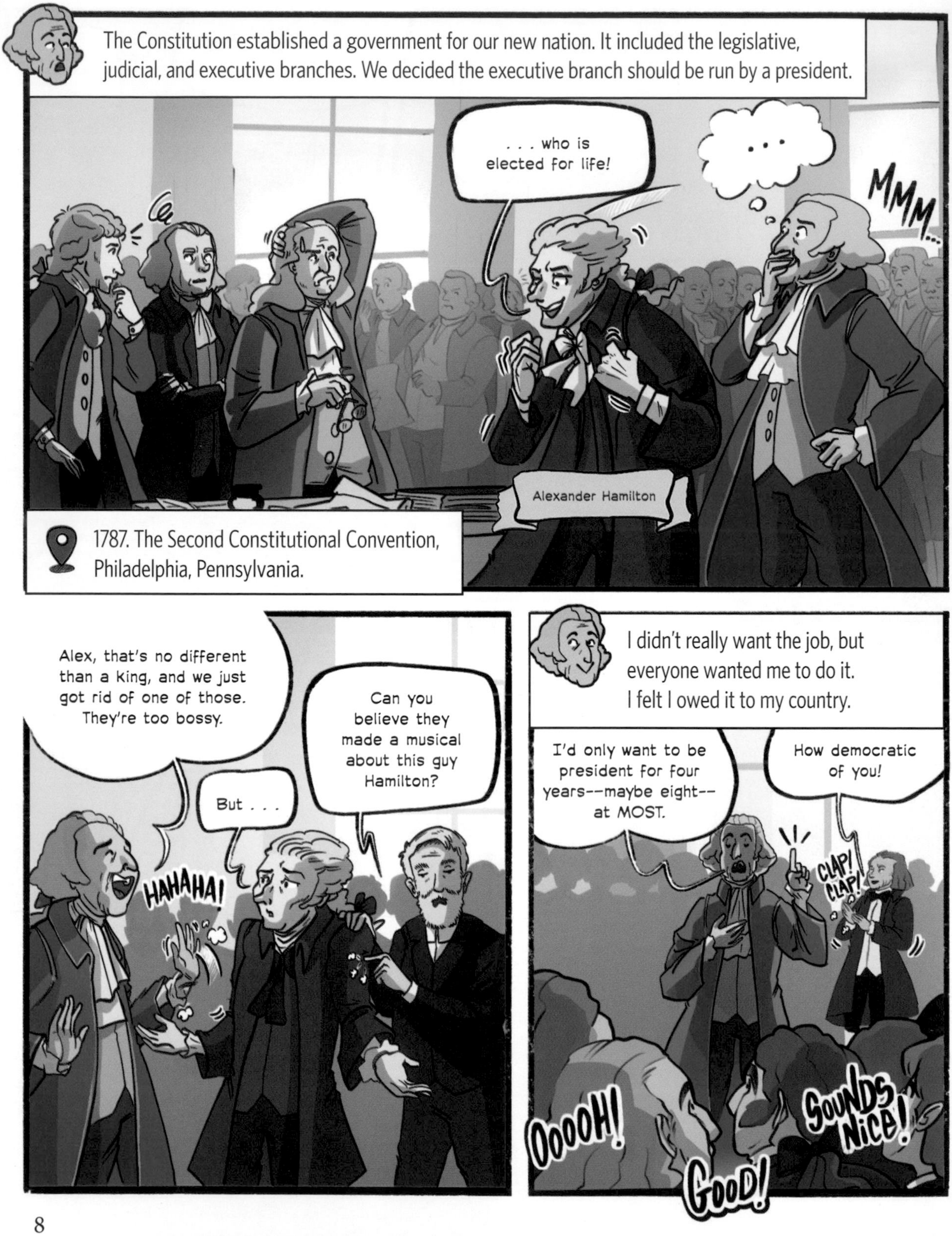
The Constitution established a government for our new nation. It included the legislative, judicial, and executive branches. We decided the executive branch should be run by a president.
. . . who is elected for life!
. . .
MMM...
Alexander Hamilton
1787. The Second Constitutional Convention, Philadelphia, Pennsylvania.
Alex, that's no different than a king, and we just got rid of one of those. They're too bossy.
But . . .
Can you believe they made a musical about this guy Hamilton?
HAHAHA!
I didn't really want the job, but everyone wanted me to do it. I felt I owed it to my country.
I'd only want to be president for four years--maybe eight--at MOST.
How democratic of you!
CLAP! CLAP!
OOOOH!
GOOD!
SOUNDS NICE!

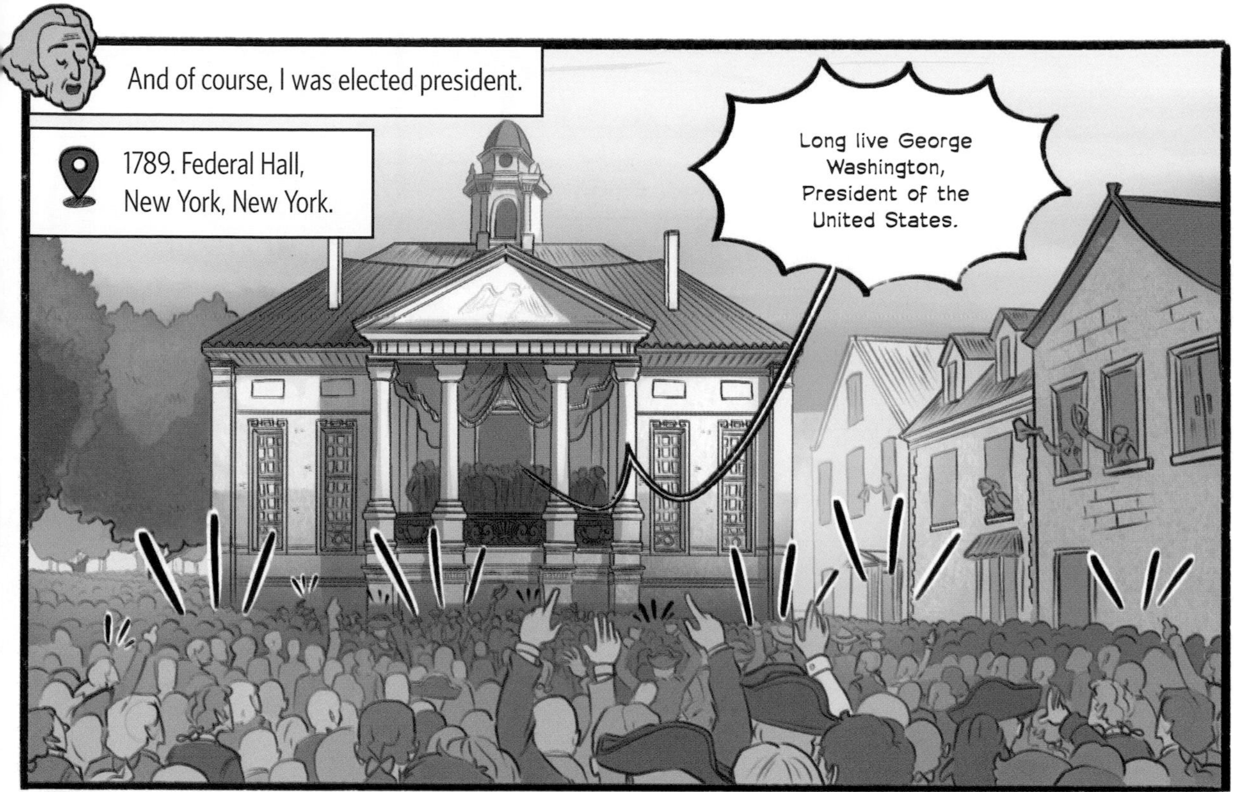
And of course, I was elected president.
1789. Federal Hall, New York, New York.
Long live George Washington, President of the United States.

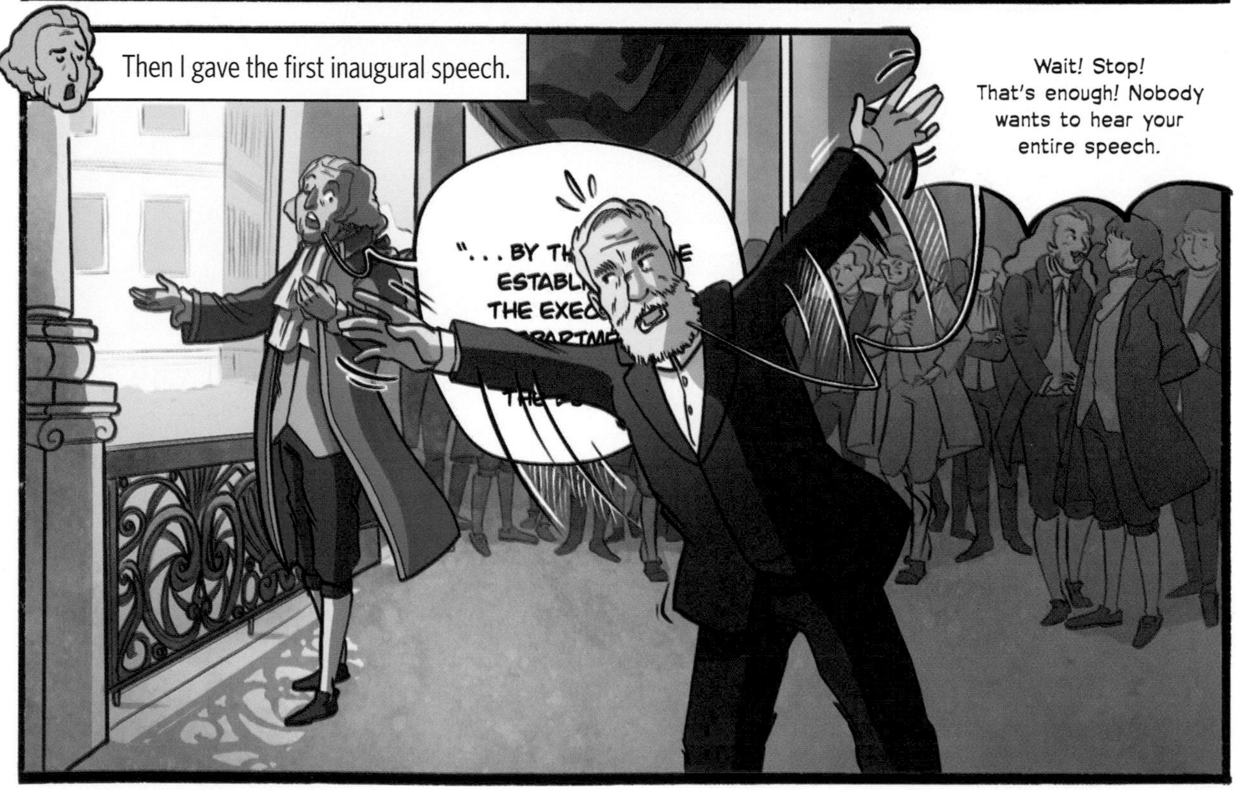
Then I gave the first inaugural speech.
Wait! Stop! That's enough! Nobody wants to hear your entire speech.

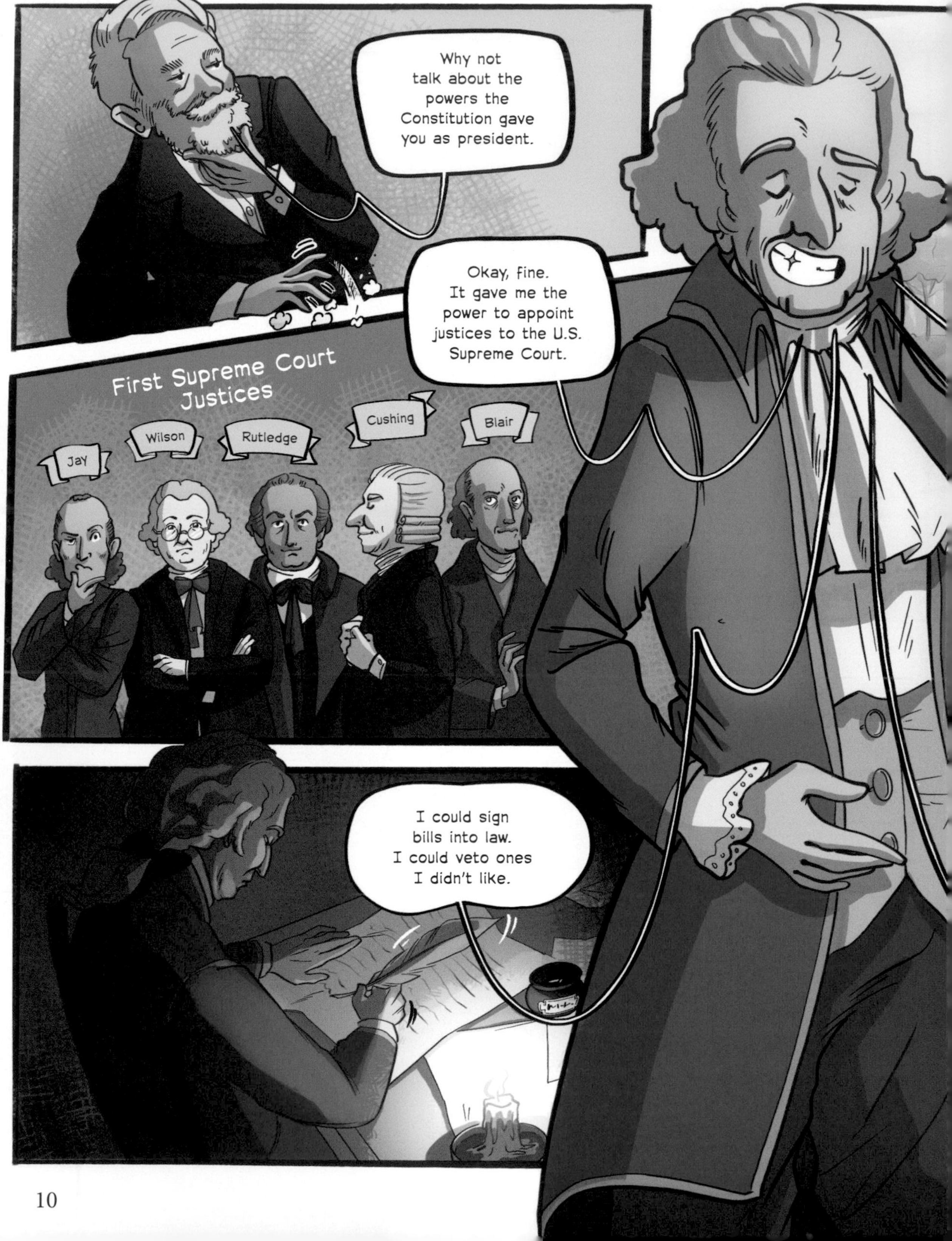
Why not talk about the powers the Constitution gave you as president.
Okay, fine. It gave me the power to appoint justices to the U.S. Supreme Court.
First Supreme Court Justices
Jay
Wilson
Rutledge
Cushing
Blair
I could sign bills into law. I could veto ones I didn't like.

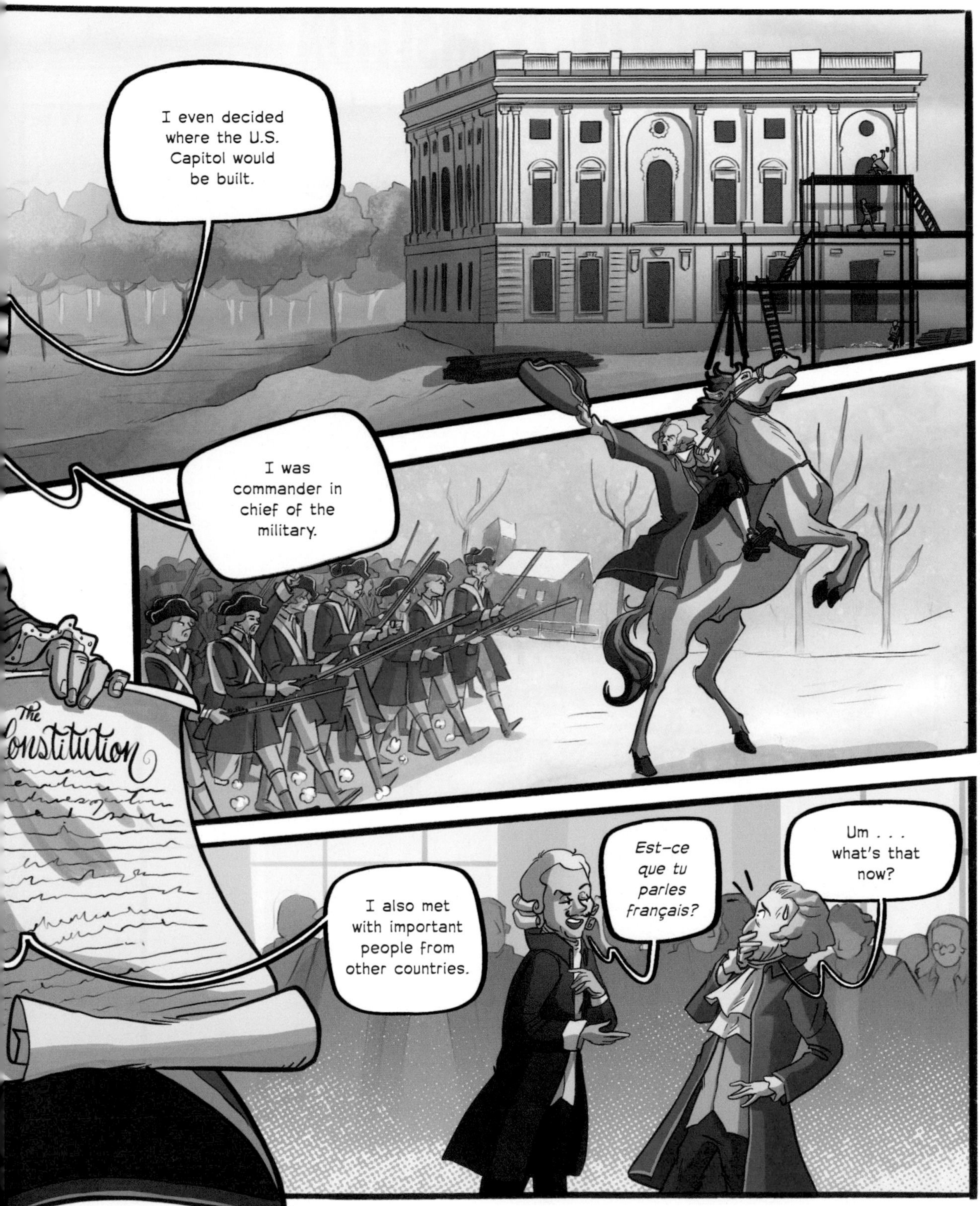
I even decided where the U.S. Capitol would be built.
I was commander in chief of the military.
The Constitution
I also met with important people from other countries.
Est-ce que tu parles français?
Um . . . what's that now?

CHAPTER TWO: A PEACEFUL TRANSITION

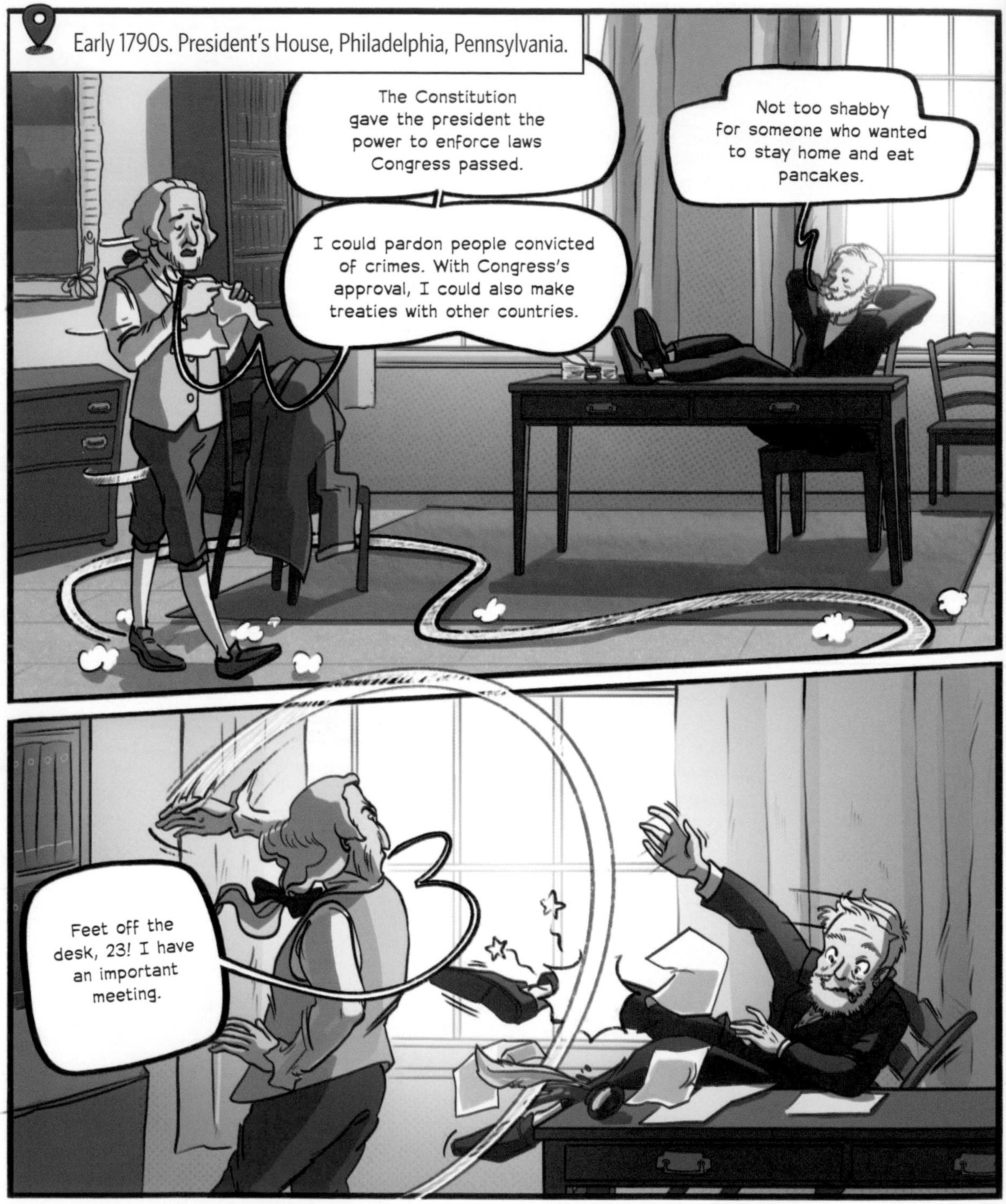
Early 1790s. President's House, Philadelphia, Pennsylvania.
The Constitution gave the president the power to enforce laws Congress passed.
I could pardon people convicted of crimes. With Congress's approval, I could also make treaties with other countries.
Not too shabby for someone who wanted to stay home and eat pancakes.
Feet off the desk, 23! I have an important meeting.

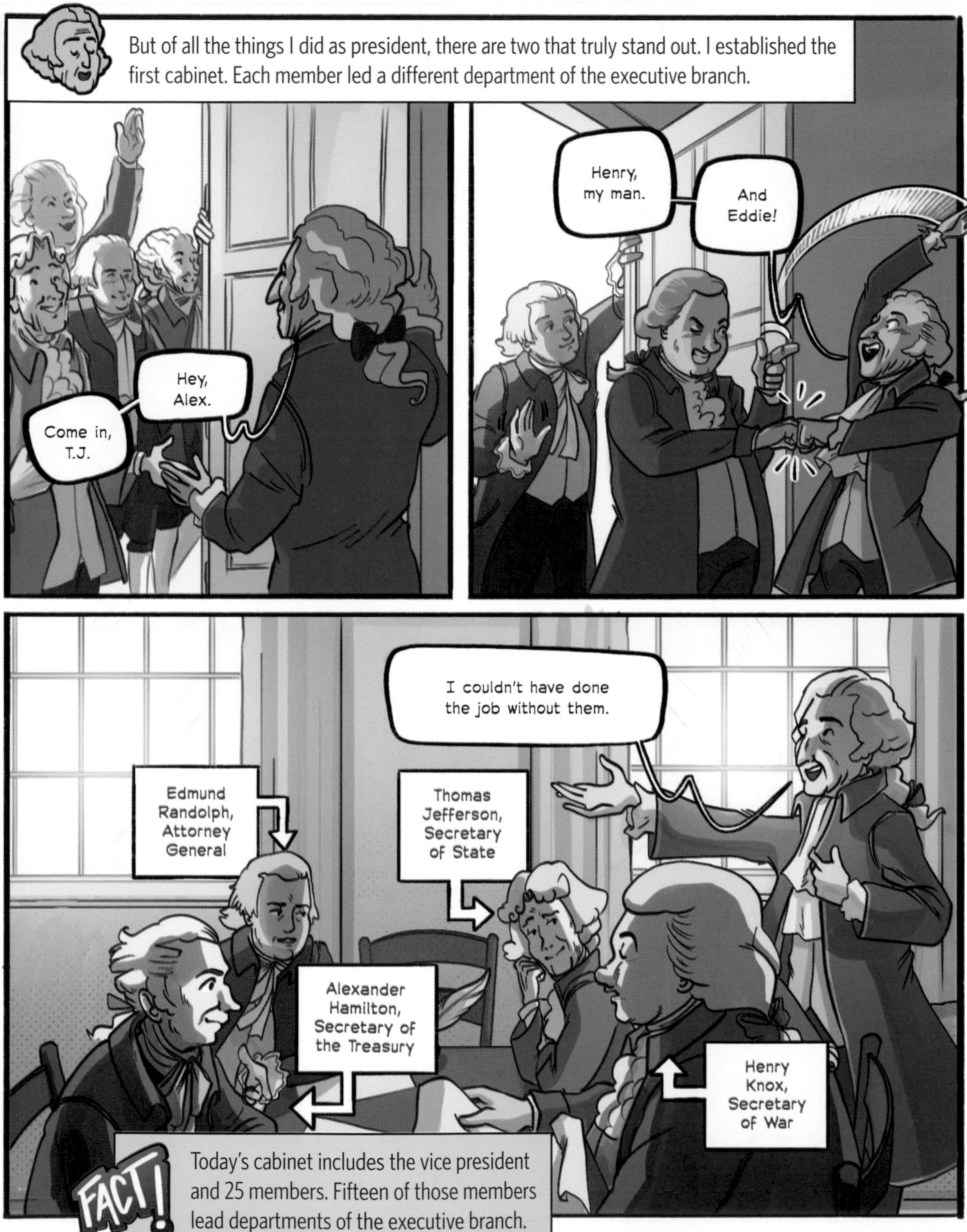

But of all the things I did as president, there are two that truly stand out. I established the first cabinet. Each member led a different department of the executive branch.
Hey, Alex.
Come in, T.J.
Henry, my man.
And Eddie!
I couldn't have done the job without them.
Edmund Randolph, Attorney General
Thomas Jefferson, Secretary of State
Alexander Hamilton, Secretary of the Treasury
Henry Knox, Secretary of War
FACT!
Today's cabinet includes the vice president and 25 members. Fifteen of those members lead departments of the executive branch.

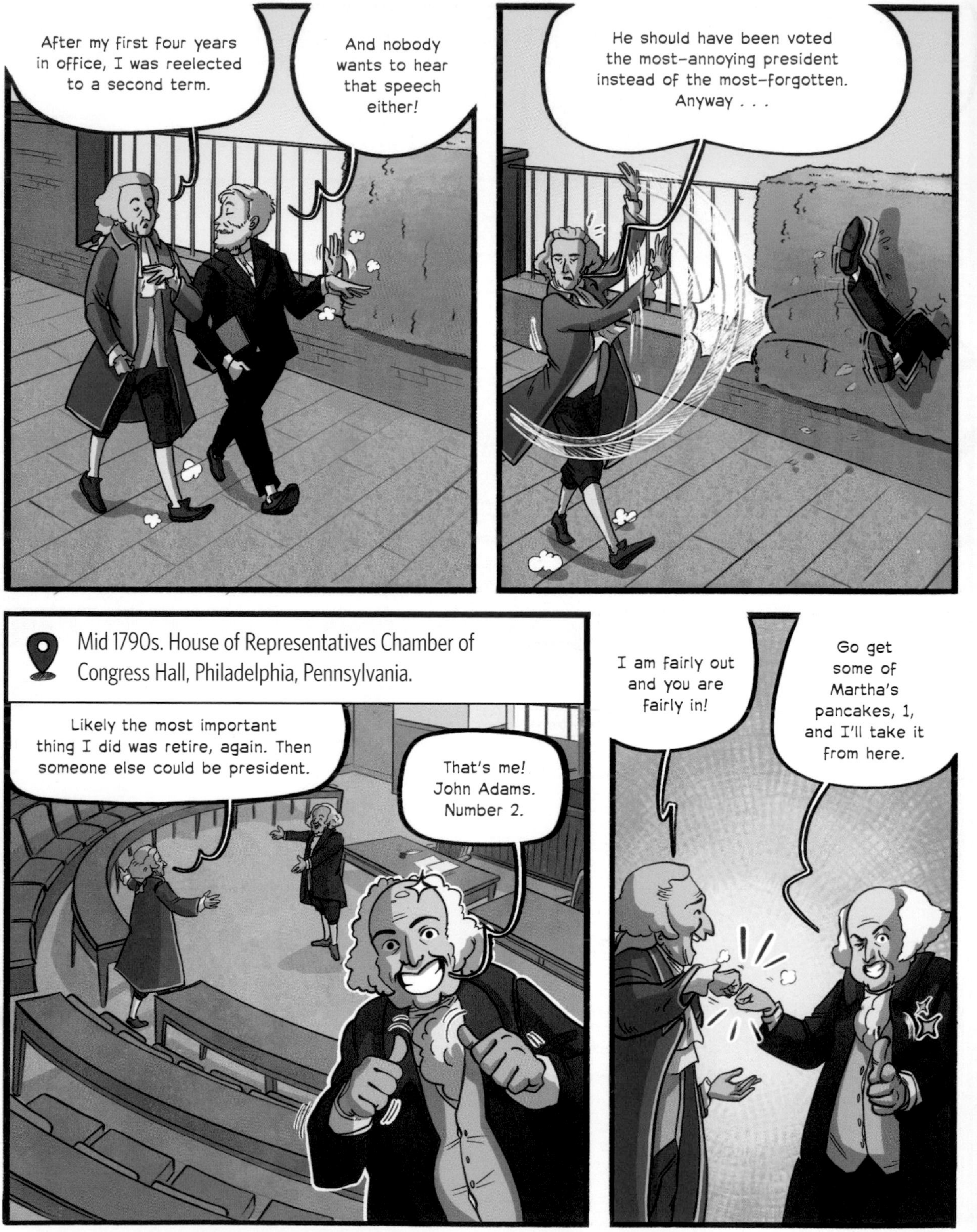
After my first four years in office, I was reelected to a second term.
And nobody wants to hear that speech either!
He should have been voted the most-annoying president instead of the most-forgotten. Anyway . . .
Mid 1790s. House of Representatives Chamber of Congress Hall, Philadelphia, Pennsylvania.
Likely the most important thing I did was retire, again. Then someone else could be president.
That's me! John Adams. Number 2.
I am fairly out and you are fairly in!
Go get some of Martha's pancakes, 1, and I'll take it from here.

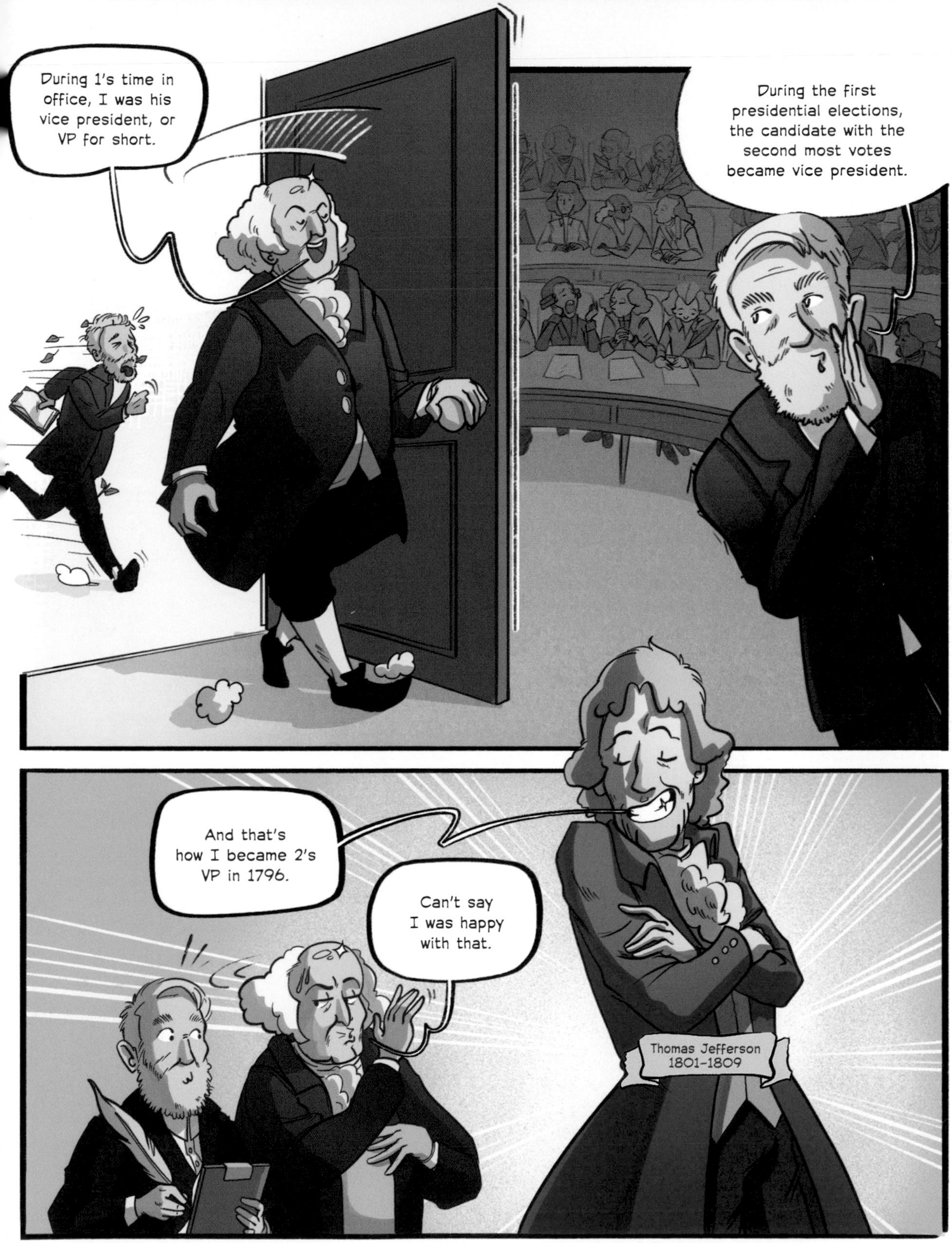
During 1's time in office, I was his vice president, or VP for short.
During the first presidential elections, the candidate with the second most votes became vice president.
And that's how I became 2's VP in 1796.
Can't say I was happy with that.
Thomas Jefferson 1801–1809

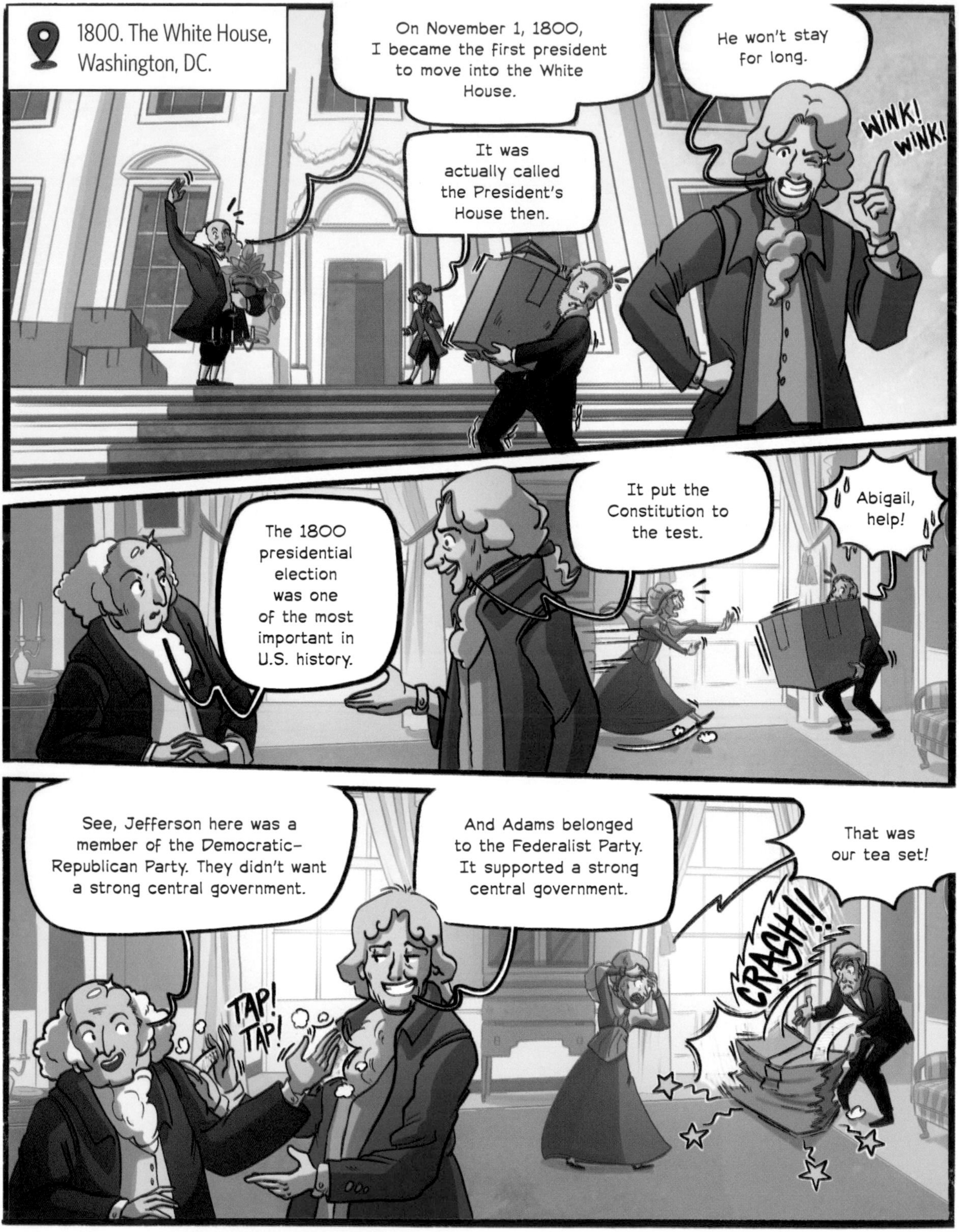
1800. The White House, Washington, DC.
On November 1, 1800, I became the first president to move into the White House.
It was actually called the President's House then.
He won't stay for long.
WINK! WINK!
The 1800 presidential election was one of the most important in U.S. history.
It put the Constitution to the test.
Abigail, help!
See, Jefferson here was a member of the Democratic-Republican Party. They didn't want a strong central government.
And Adams belonged to the Federalist Party. It supported a strong central government.
TAP! TAP!
That was our tea set!
CRASH!!

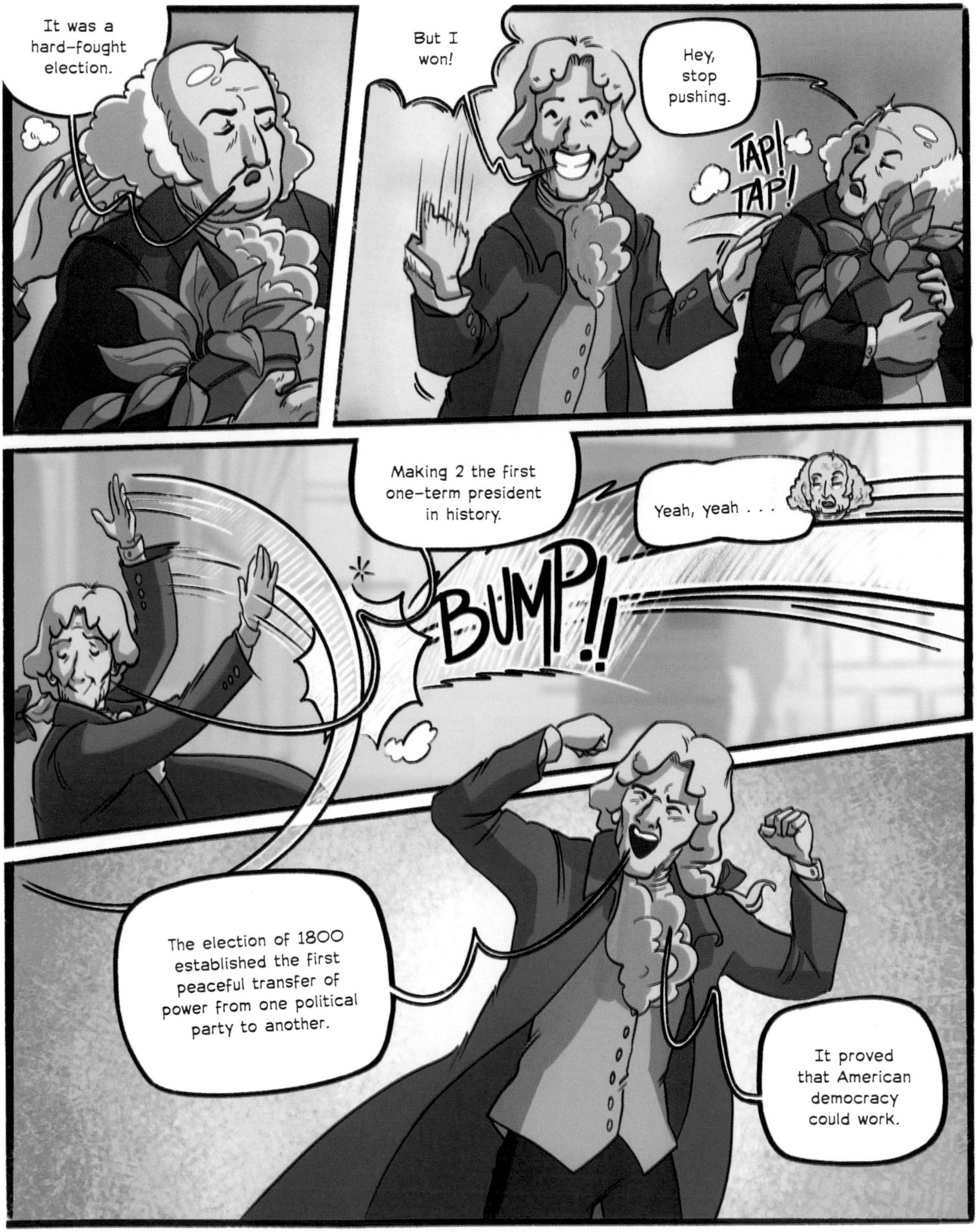

It was a hard-fought election.
But I won!
Hey, stop pushing.
TAP! TAP!
Making 2 the first one-term president in history.
Yeah, yeah . . .
BUMP!!
The election of 1800 established the first peaceful transfer of power from one political party to another.
It proved that American democracy could work.

CHAPTER THREE: THE ROLE OF THE PRESIDENT

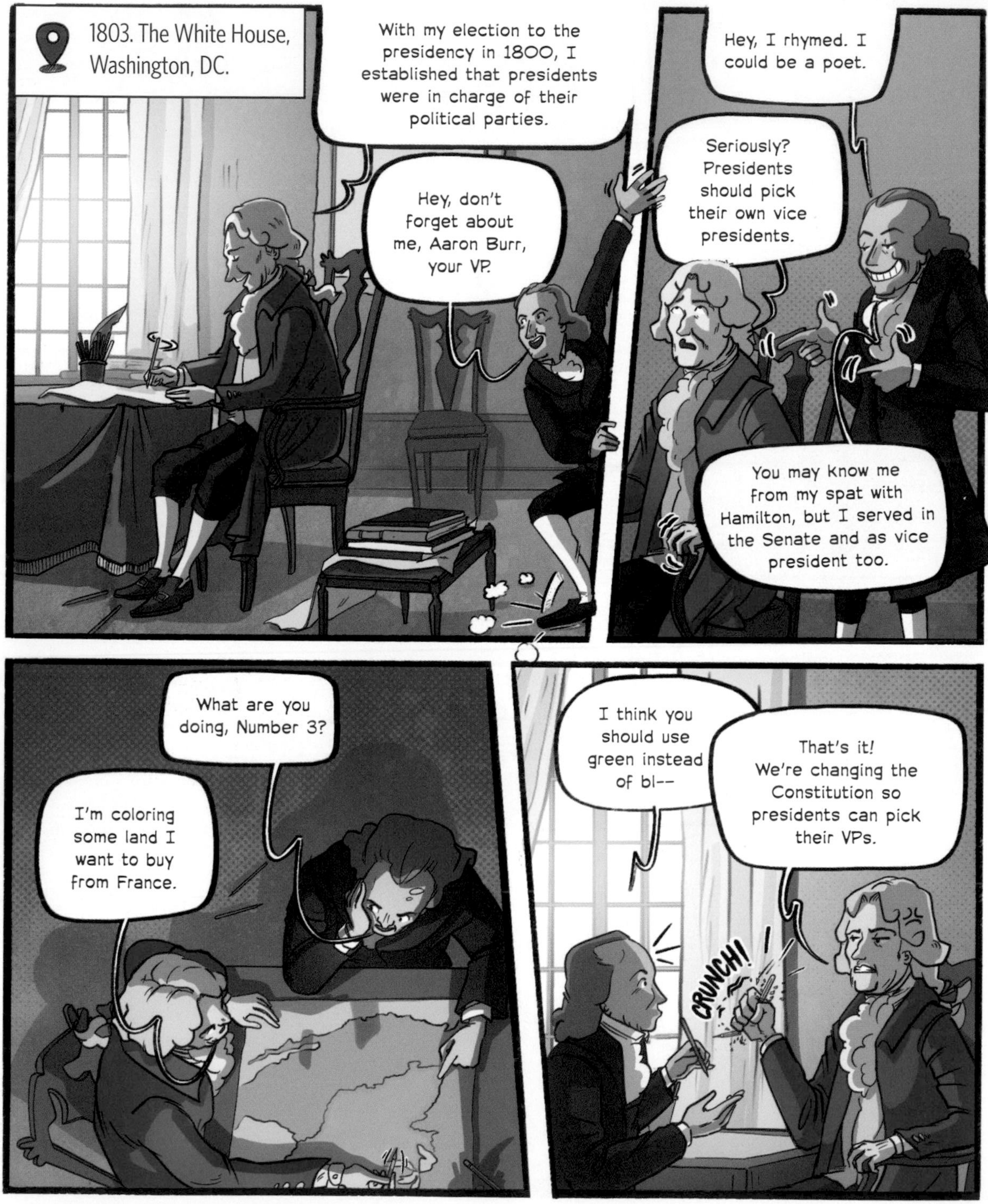
1803. The White House, Washington, DC.
With my election to the presidency in 1800, I established that presidents were in charge of their political parties.
Hey, don't forget about me, Aaron Burr, your VP.
Hey, I rhymed. I could be a poet.
Seriously? Presidents should pick their own vice presidents.
You may know me from my spat with Hamilton, but I served in the Senate and as vice president too.
What are you doing, Number 3?
I'm coloring some land I want to buy from France.
I think you should use green instead of bl--
That's it! We're changing the Constitution so presidents can pick their VPs.
CRUNCH!

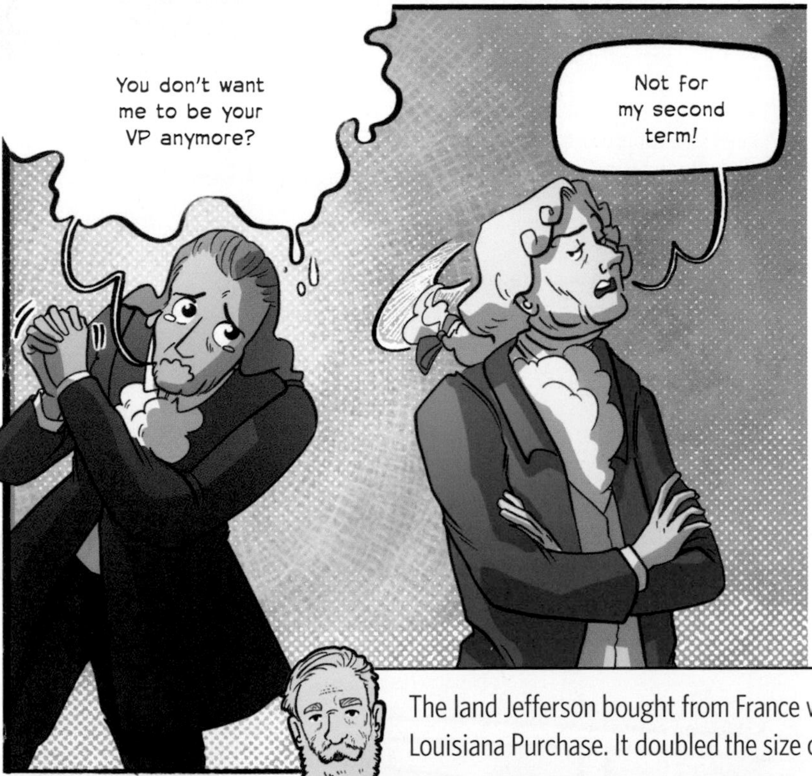
You don't want me to be your VP anymore?
Not for my second term!

RUNNING PARTNERS

The Twelfth Amendment states that the president and vice president will be elected together. It was approved or "ratified" on June 15, 1804, months before Jefferson was elected to a second term. He chose George Clinton, one of the Founding Fathers.

The land Jefferson bought from France was known as the Louisiana Purchase. It doubled the size of the country.

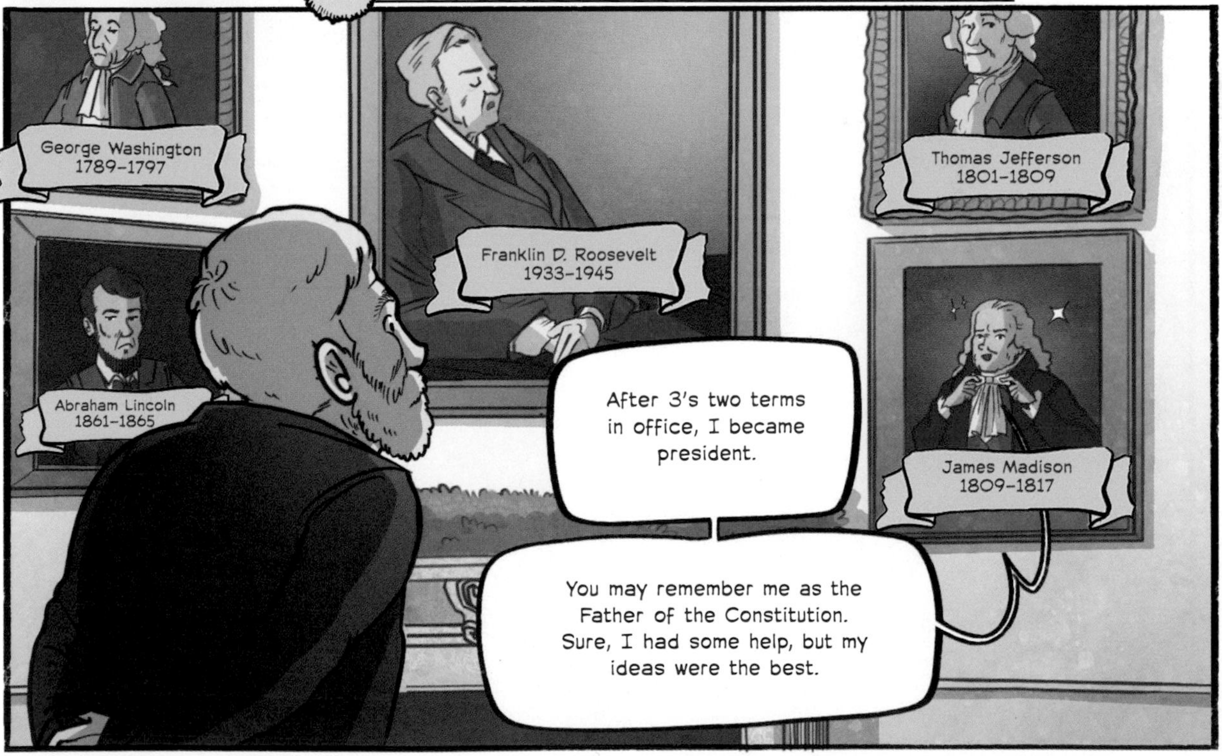
George Washington 1789–1797
Franklin D. Roosevelt 1933–1945
Thomas Jefferson 1801–1809
Abraham Lincoln 1861–1865
James Madison 1809–1817
After 3's two terms in office, I became president.
You may remember me as the Father of the Constitution. Sure, I had some help, but my ideas were the best.

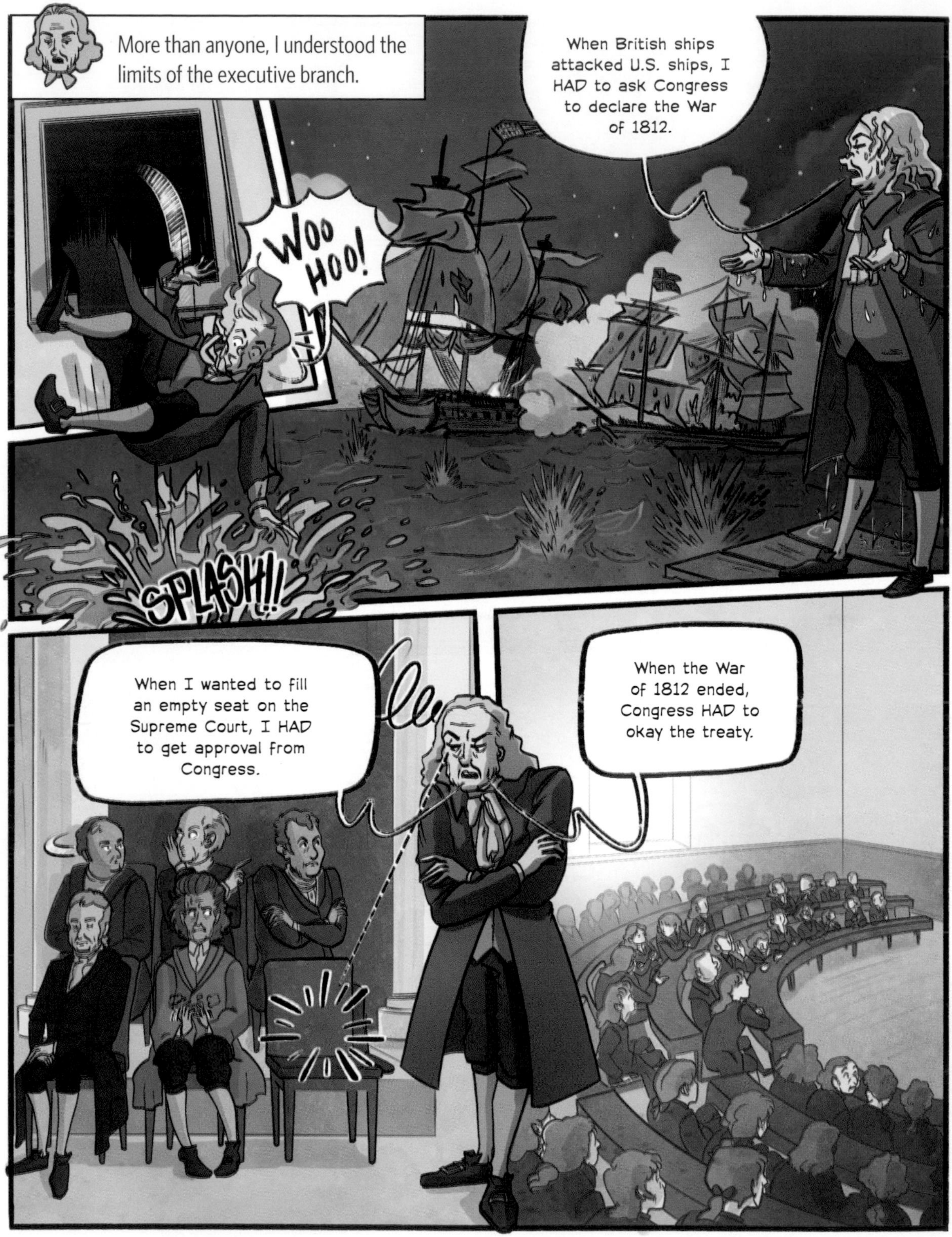
More than anyone, I understood the limits of the executive branch.
When British ships attacked U.S. ships, I HAD to ask Congress to declare the War of 1812.
WOO HOO!
SPLASH!!!
When I wanted to fill an empty seat on the Supreme Court, I HAD to get approval from Congress.
When the War of 1812 ended, Congress HAD to okay the treaty.

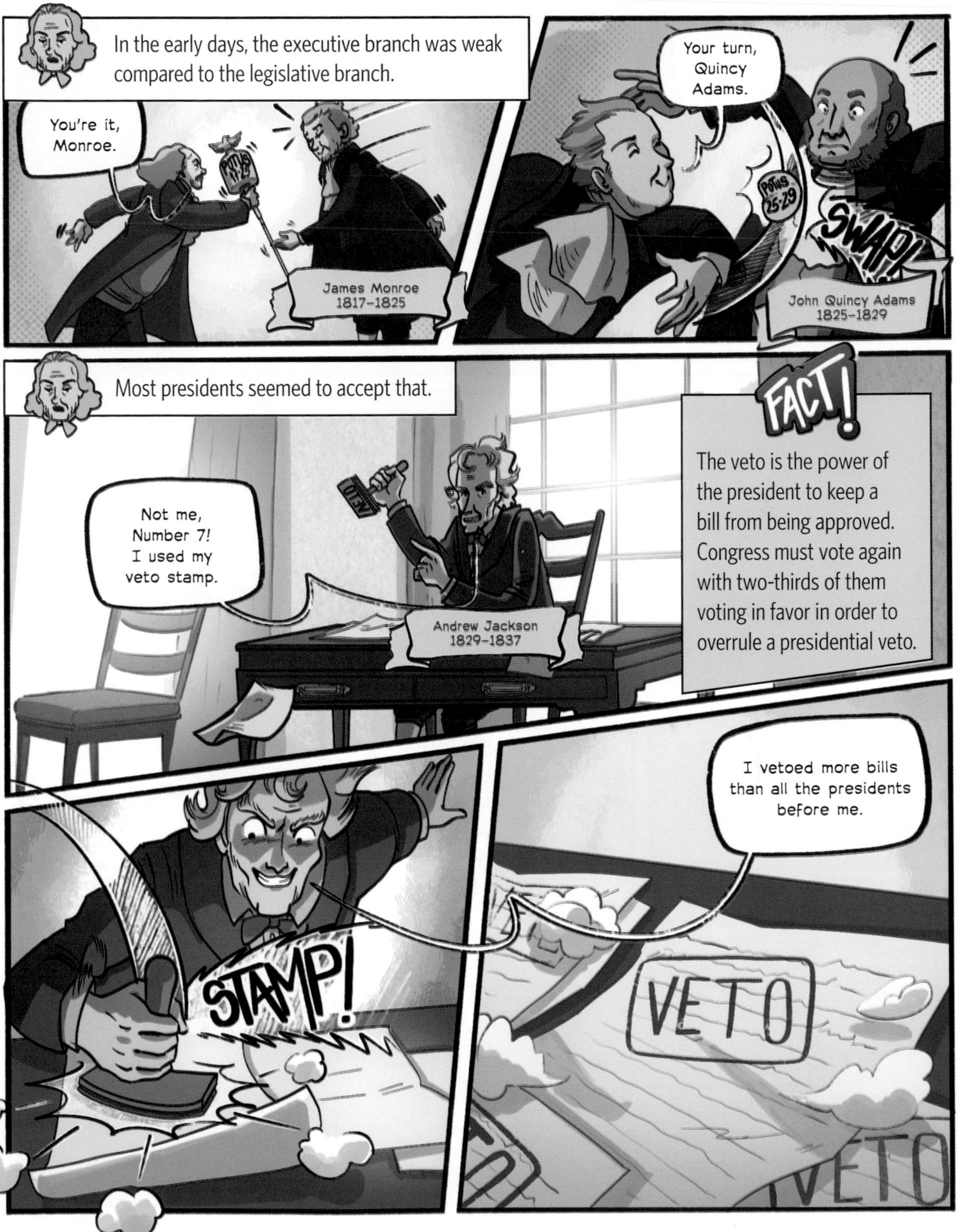
In the early days, the executive branch was weak compared to the legislative branch.
You're it, Monroe.
POTUS 17-25
James Monroe 1817–1825
Your turn, Quincy Adams.
POTUS 25-29
SWAP!
John Quincy Adams 1825–1829
Most presidents seemed to accept that.
Not me, Number 7! I used my veto stamp.
Andrew Jackson 1829–1837
FACT!
The veto is the power of the president to keep a bill from being approved. Congress must vote again with two-thirds of them voting in favor in order to overrule a presidential veto.
STAMP!
I vetoed more bills than all the presidents before me.
VETO
VETO

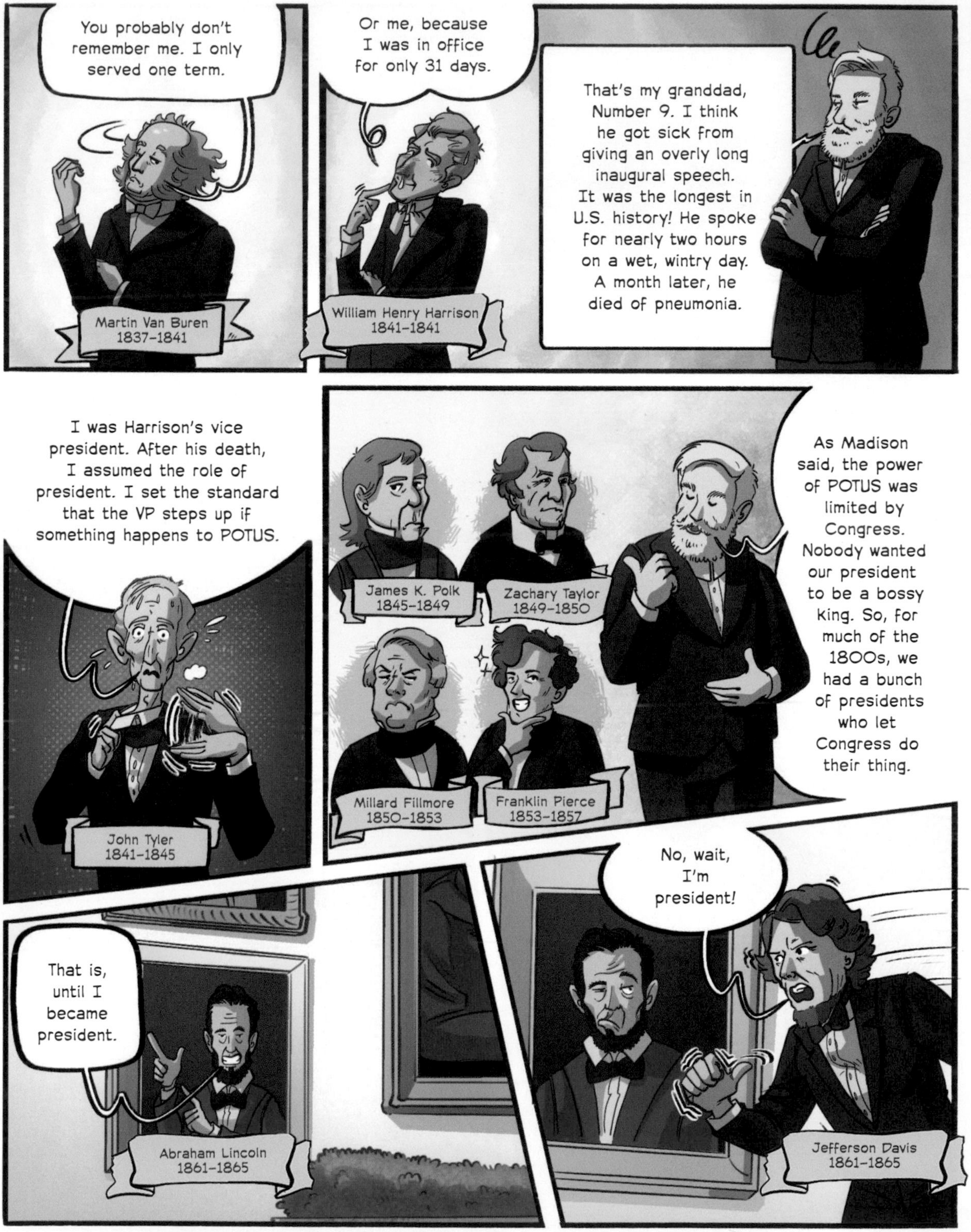

You probably don't remember me. I only served one term.
Martin Van Buren 1837–1841
Or me, because I was in office for only 31 days.
William Henry Harrison 1841–1841
That's my granddad, Number 9. I think he got sick from giving an overly long inaugural speech. It was the longest in U.S. history! He spoke for nearly two hours on a wet, wintry day. A month later, he died of pneumonia.
I was Harrison's vice president. After his death, I assumed the role of president. I set the standard that the VP steps up if something happens to POTUS.
John Tyler 1841–1845
James K. Polk 1845–1849
Zachary Taylor 1849–1850
Millard Fillmore 1850–1853
Franklin Pierce 1853–1857
As Madison said, the power of POTUS was limited by Congress. Nobody wanted our president to be a bossy king. So, for much of the 1800s, we had a bunch of presidents who let Congress do their thing.
That is, until I became president.
Abraham Lincoln 1861–1865
No, wait, I'm president!
Jefferson Davis 1861–1865

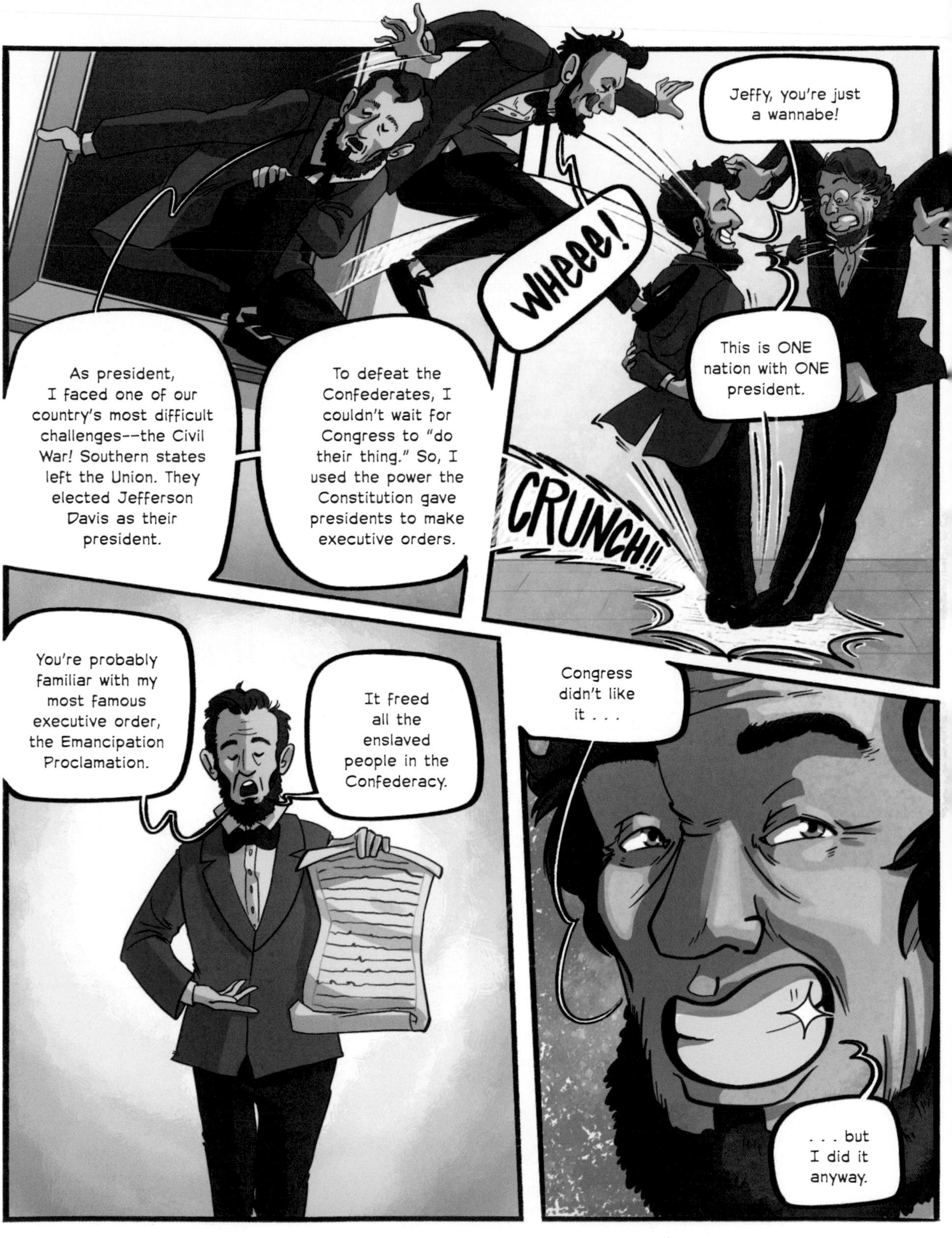
As president, I faced one of our country's most difficult challenges--the Civil War! Southern states left the Union. They elected Jefferson Davis as their president.
To defeat the Confederates, I couldn't wait for Congress to "do their thing." So, I used the power the Constitution gave presidents to make executive orders.
WHEEE!
Jeffy, you're just a wannabe!
This is ONE nation with ONE president.
CRUNCH!!
You're probably familiar with my most famous executive order, the Emancipation Proclamation.
It freed all the enslaved people in the Confederacy.
Congress didn't like it . . .
. . . but I did it anyway.

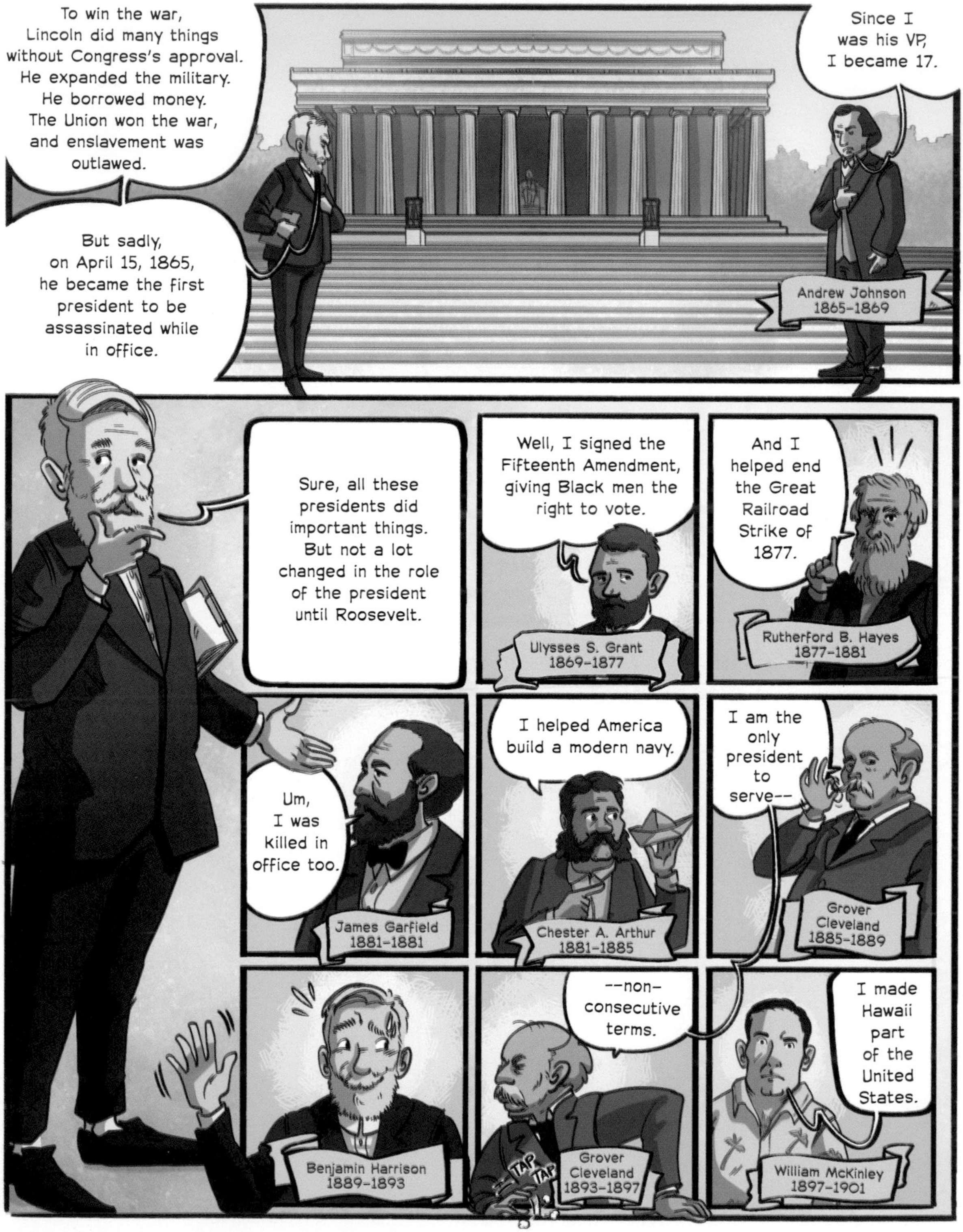
To win the war, Lincoln did many things without Congress's approval. He expanded the military. He borrowed money. The Union won the war, and enslavement was outlawed.
Since I was his VP, I became 17.
But sadly, on April 15, 1865, he became the first president to be assassinated while in office.
Andrew Johnson 1865–1869
Sure, all these presidents did important things. But not a lot changed in the role of the president until Roosevelt.
Well, I signed the Fifteenth Amendment, giving Black men the right to vote.
Ulysses S. Grant 1869–1877
And I helped end the Great Railroad Strike of 1877.
Rutherford B. Hayes 1877–1881
Um, I was killed in office too.
James Garfield 1881–1881
I helped America build a modern navy.
Chester A. Arthur 1881–1885
I am the only president to serve--
Grover Cleveland 1885–1889
Benjamin Harrison 1889–1893
--non-consecutive terms.
TAP TAP
Grover Cleveland 1893–1897
I made Hawaii part of the United States.
William McKinley 1897–1901

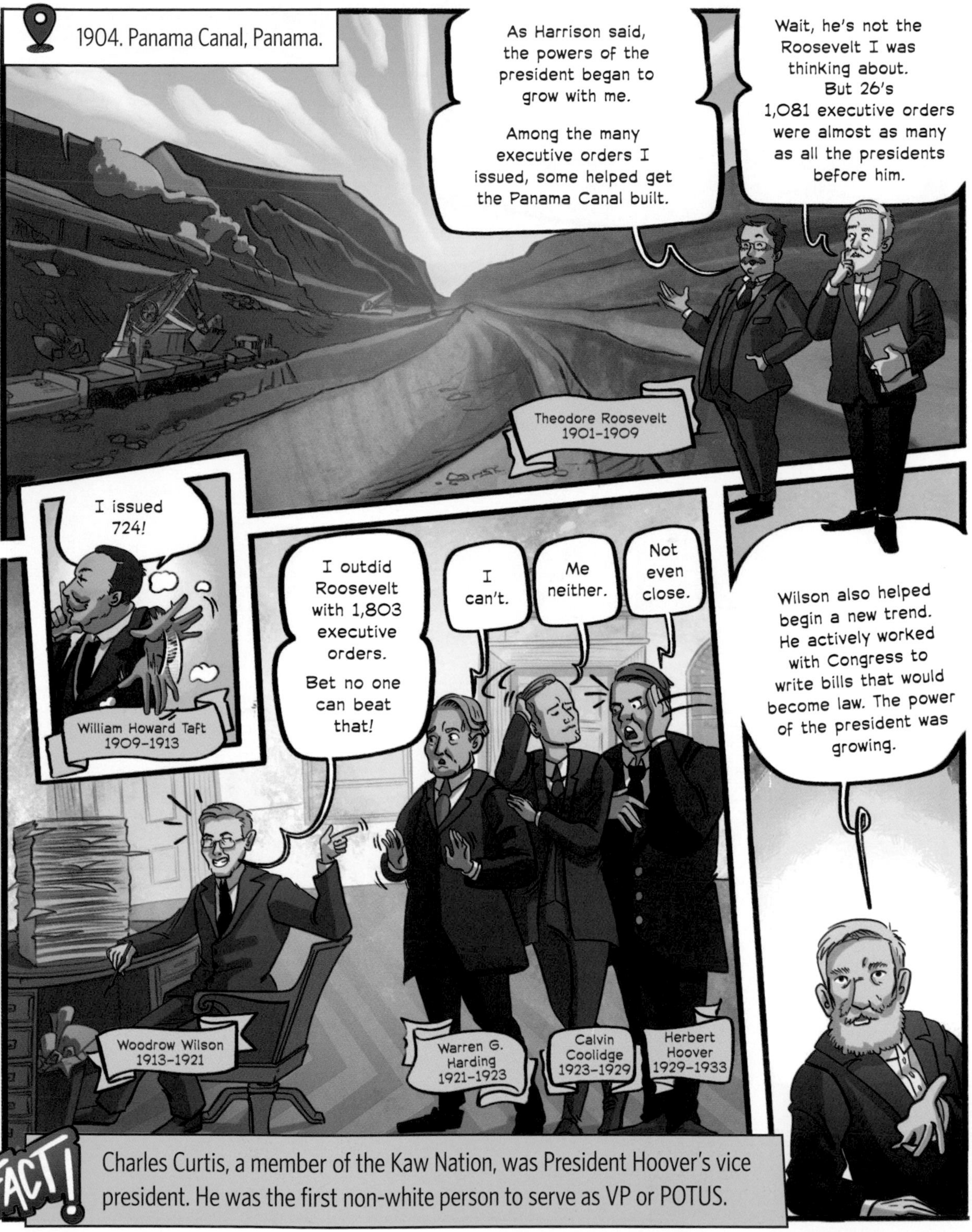
1904. Panama Canal, Panama.
As Harrison said, the powers of the president began to grow with me.
Among the many executive orders I issued, some helped get the Panama Canal built.
Wait, he's not the Roosevelt I was thinking about. But 26's 1,081 executive orders were almost as many as all the presidents before him.
Theodore Roosevelt 1901–1909
I issued 724!
William Howard Taft 1909–1913
I outdid Roosevelt with 1,803 executive orders.
Bet no one can beat that!
I can't.
Me neither.
Not even close.
Wilson also helped begin a new trend. He actively worked with Congress to write bills that would become law. The power of the president was growing.
Woodrow Wilson 1913–1921
Warren G. Harding 1921–1923
Calvin Coolidge 1923–1929
Herbert Hoover 1929–1933

FACT! Charles Curtis, a member of the Kaw Nation, was President Hoover's vice president. He was the first non-white person to serve as VP or POTUS.

CHAPTER FOUR: MODERN PRESIDENTS

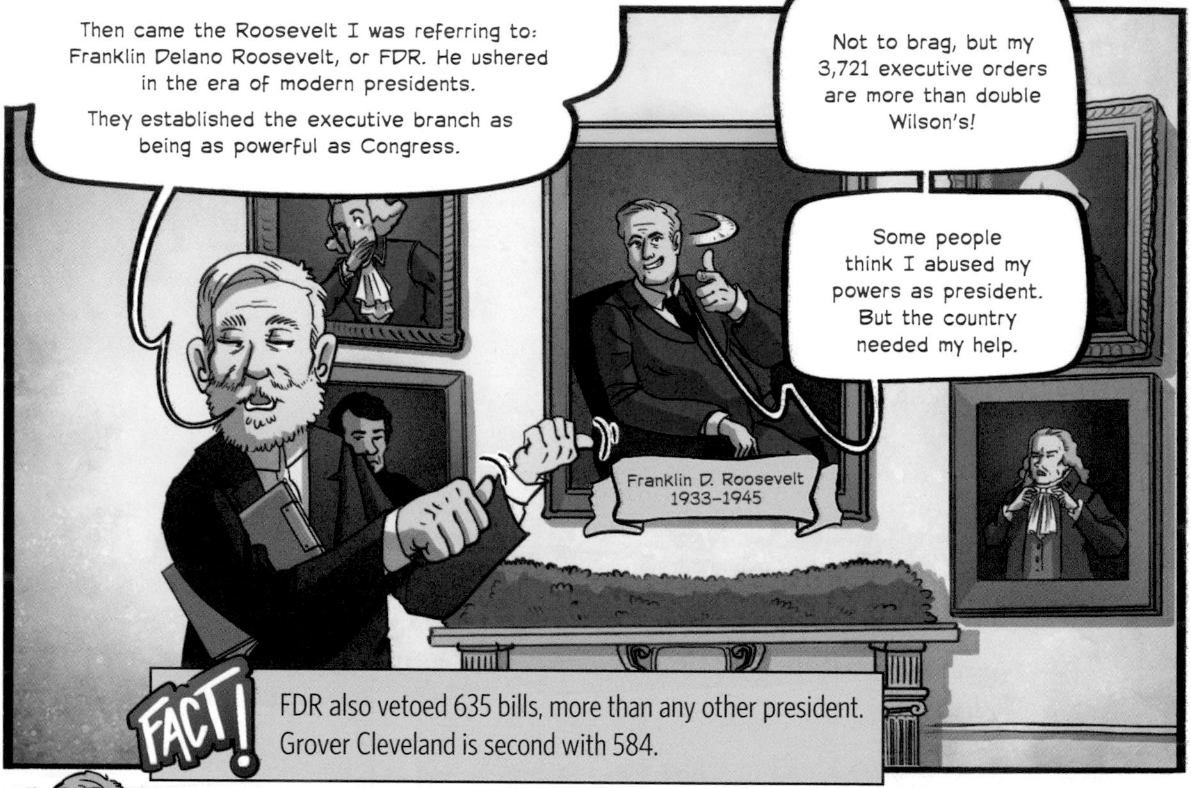
Then came the Roosevelt I was referring to: Franklin Delano Roosevelt, or FDR. He ushered in the era of modern presidents.
They established the executive branch as being as powerful as Congress.
Not to brag, but my 3,721 executive orders are more than double Wilson's!
Some people think I abused my powers as president. But the country needed my help.
Franklin D. Roosevelt 1933–1945
FACT!
FDR also vetoed 635 bills, more than any other president. Grover Cleveland is second with 584.

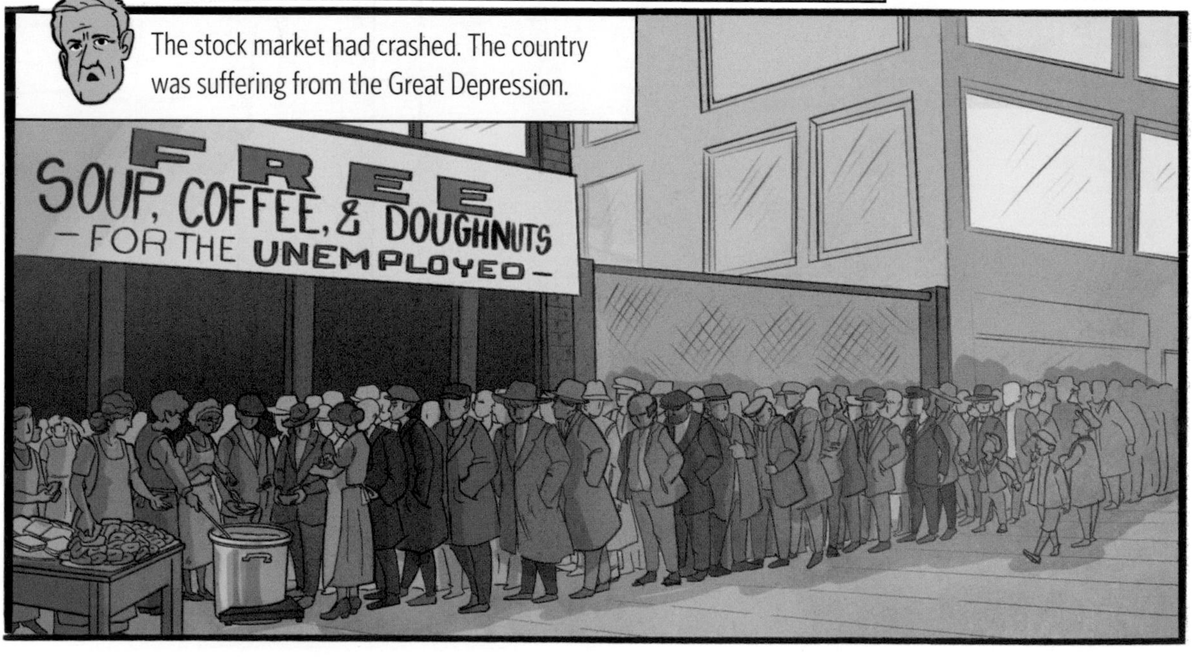
The stock market had crashed. The country was suffering from the Great Depression.
FREE SOUP, COFFEE, & DOUGHNUTS
– FOR THE UNEMPLOYED –

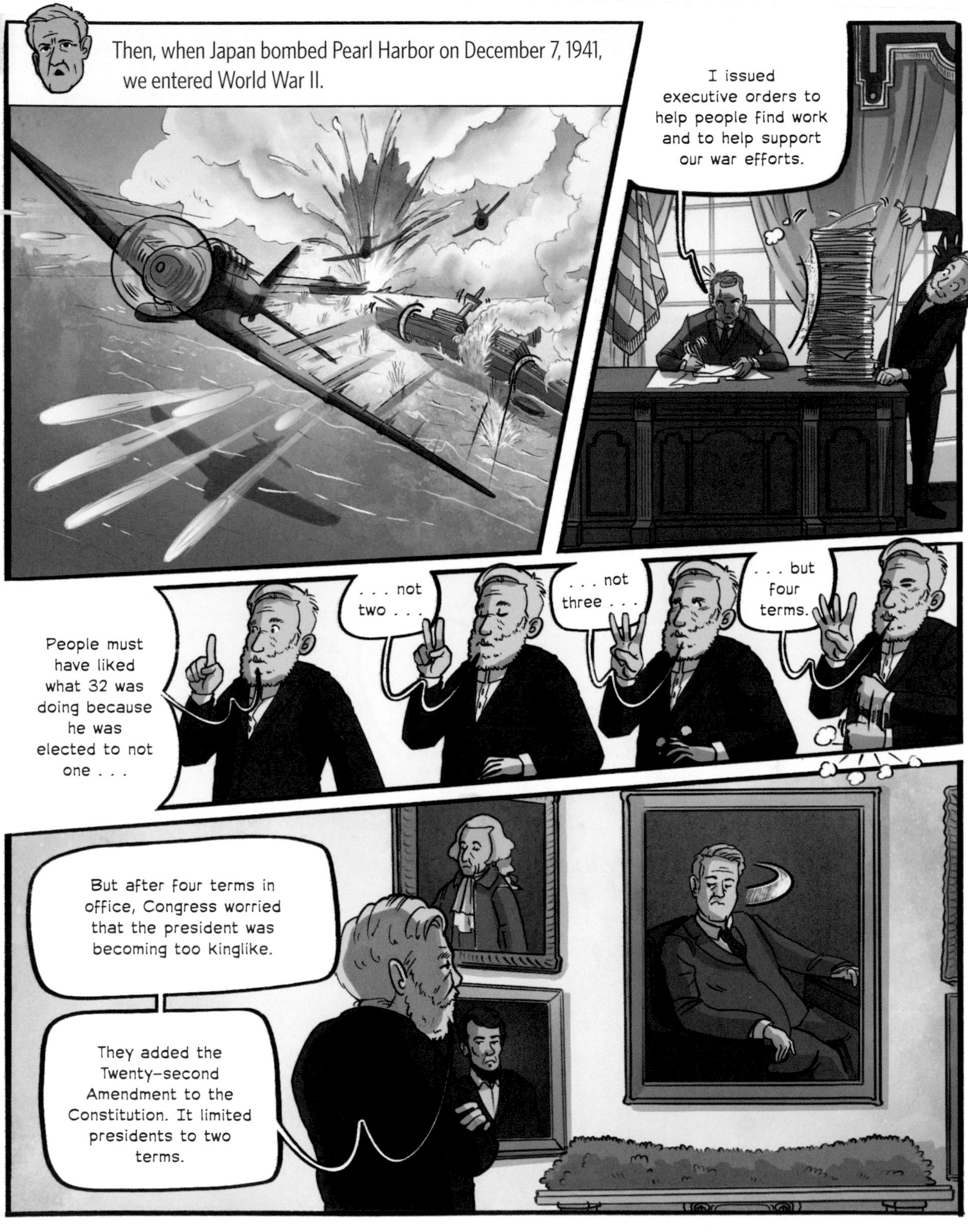

Then, when Japan bombed Pearl Harbor on December 7, 1941, we entered World War II.
I issued executive orders to help people find work and to help support our war efforts.
People must have liked what 32 was doing because he was elected to not one . . .
. . . not two . . .
. . . not three . . .
. . . but four terms.
But after four terms in office, Congress worried that the president was becoming too kinglike.
They added the Twenty-second Amendment to the Constitution. It limited presidents to two terms.

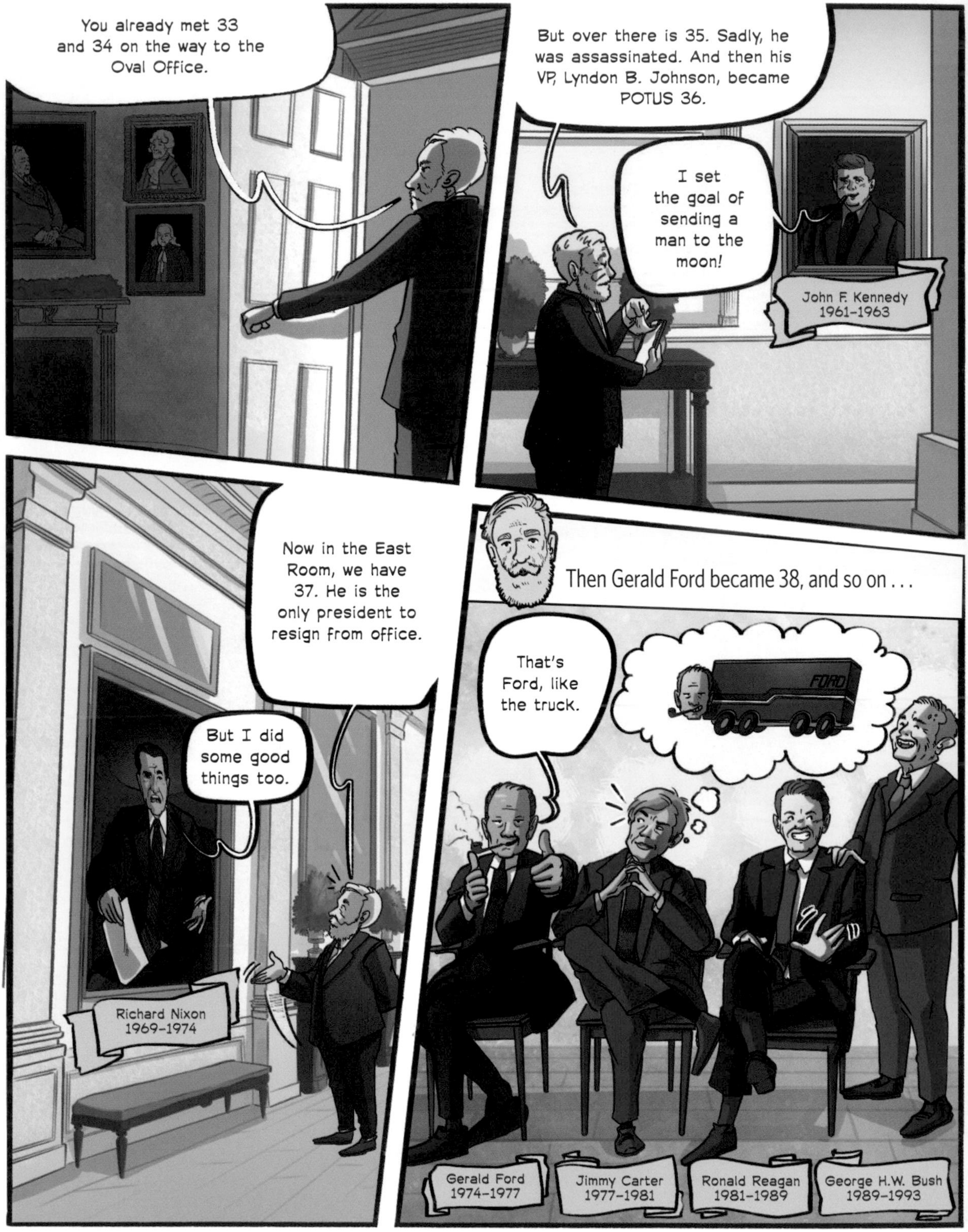
You already met 33 and 34 on the way to the Oval Office.
But over there is 35. Sadly, he was assassinated. And then his VP, Lyndon B. Johnson, became POTUS 36.
I set the goal of sending a man to the moon!
John F. Kennedy 1961–1963
Now in the East Room, we have 37. He is the only president to resign from office.
But I did some good things too.
Richard Nixon 1969–1974
Then Gerald Ford became 38, and so on . . .
That's Ford, like the truck.
FORD
Gerald Ford 1974–1977
Jimmy Carter 1977–1981
Ronald Reagan 1981–1989
George H.W. Bush 1989–1993

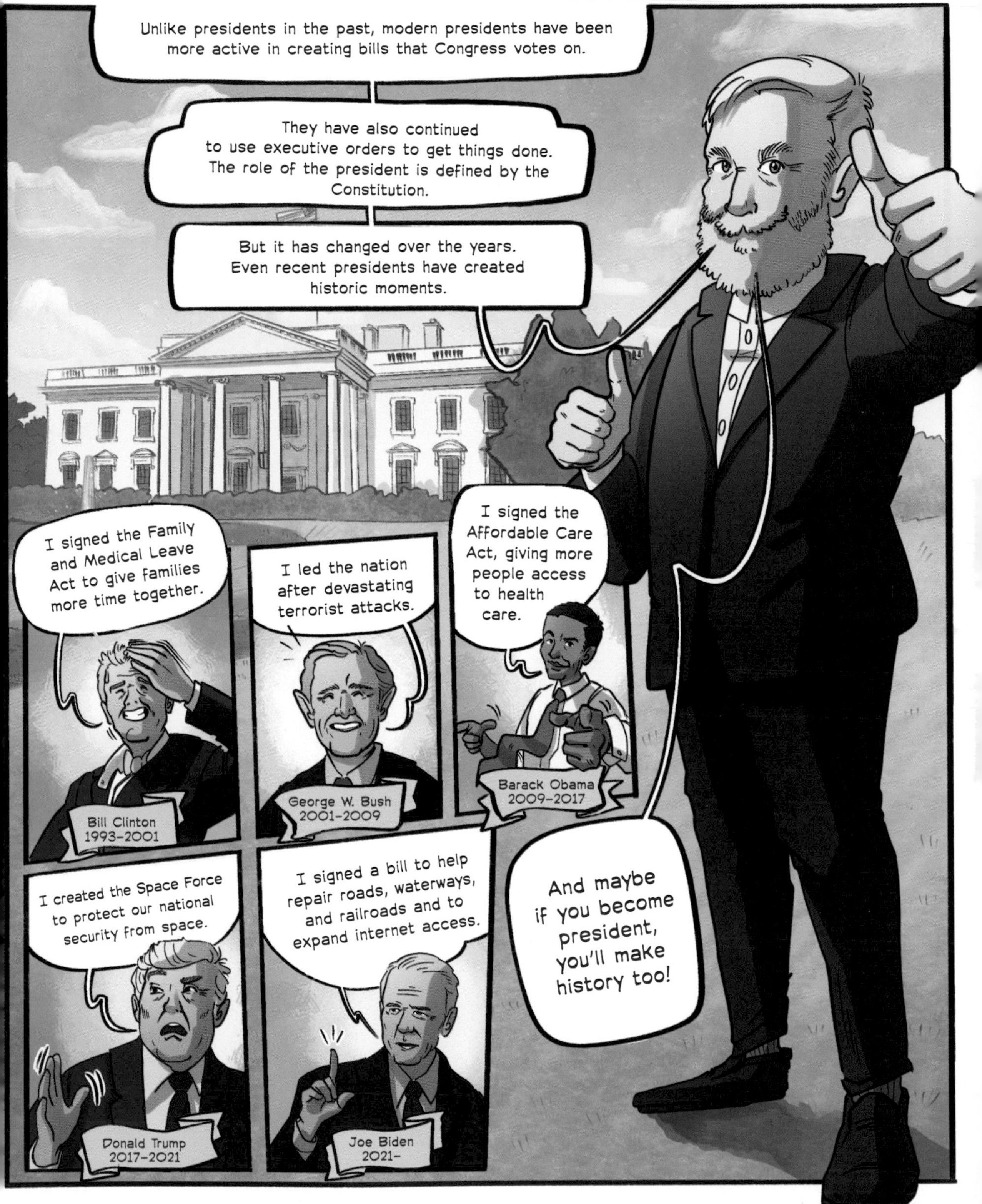
Unlike presidents in the past, modern presidents have been more active in creating bills that Congress votes on.
They have also continued to use executive orders to get things done. The role of the president is defined by the Constitution.
But it has changed over the years. Even recent presidents have created historic moments.
I signed the Family and Medical Leave Act to give families more time together.
Bill Clinton 1993–2001
I led the nation after devastating terrorist attacks.
George W. Bush 2001–2009
I signed the Affordable Care Act, giving more people access to health care.
Barack Obama 2009–2017
I created the Space Force to protect our national security from space.
Donald Trump 2017–2021
I signed a bill to help repair roads, waterways, and railroads and to expand internet access.
Joe Biden 2021–
And maybe if you become president, you'll make history too!

GLOSSARY

amendment (uh-MEND-muhnt)—a formal change made to a law or legal document, such as the U.S. Constitution

assassinate (uh-SASS-uh-nayt)—to murder a person who is well-known by secret or sudden attack, often for political reasons

bill (BIL)—a proposed law introduced in Congress

candidate (KAN-duh-dayt)—a person who runs for office, such as president

convicted (kahn-VIK-tuhd)—to be found guilty of a crime

democracy (di-MAH-kruh-see)—a form of government in which the people elect their leaders

inaugural (in-AW-ger-ul)—describes an event, such as a speech, marking the beginning of a person's time in office

justice (JUHSS-tiss)—a judge in a court of law

pardon (PAHR-duhn)—an act of official forgiveness for a serious offense

resign (ri-ZINE)—to give up a job, position, or office

retire (ri-TIRE)—to give up a line of work

veto (VEE-toh)—to refuse to approve something from becoming a law; a president has the power to veto laws they do not support

READ MORE

Knopp, Ezra E. *Myths and Facts about George Washington*. Buffalo, NY: PowerKids Press, 2024.

McDonnell, Julia. *How Are Laws Made?* New York: Gareth Stevens Publishing, 2022.

Taylor, Charlotte. *The Truth about the Constitutional Convention*. New York: Enslow Publishing, 2023.

INTERNET SITES

Constitution Annotated
constitution.congress.gov

Harry S. Truman Library & Museum/Keeping the Balance: What a President Can Do and Cannot Do
trumanlibrary.gov/education/three-branches/what-president-can-do-cannot-do

The White House: Presidents
whitehouse.gov/about-the-white-house/presidents/

ABOUT THE AUTHOR

Blake Hoena grew up in central Wisconsin, and he is old enough to remember when Gerald Ford became president. He was camping with his grandparents, and everyone joked that Grandpa Hoena's pickup was a Ford, just like the president! Blake now lives in Minnesota and writes about fun things like space aliens and superheroes and sometimes even history. He has written more than 100 chapter books and graphic novels for children.

ABOUT THE ILLUSTRATOR

Manuel Molvar was born in Seville, Spain. He has been drawing ever since he can remember, which led him to get a degree in Fine Arts. Recently, Manu moved to Barcelona to study illustration. There he works as an illustrator and graphic designer. Drawing is his favorite way of expression. Manu's style is influenced by the anime and cartoons he loved as a child, mixed with the style and traditions of southern Spain.